FLASHES OF GLORY

Showing Science and the Bible both as correct; evolution wrong!

CHRIS DOREAN

FLASHES OF GLORY
Showing Science and the Bible both as correct; evolution wrong!
by Chris Dorean

Printed in the United States of America

ISBN 9781498422109

www.xulonpress.com

Revealing the truth of both Science and the Bible, but not evolution!

Disclaimer

CONTENTS

INTRODUCTION: CHALLENGING A GIANT! vii

1. ONE FACT CHANGES ALL! 11

2. SCIENCE, ENERGY, AND... ATOMS!. 24

3. LOVE AS ARCHITECT!. 31

4. THERMO-DYNAMICS; SCIENCE UNDERSCORES THE CURSE ON SIN!. . . 55

5. FLASHES OF GLORY! 66

6. THE GENETIC CODE! 99

7. TIME AND ETERNITY! 115

8. THE EARTH IS YOUNG! 139

9. ENERGY, TWO TREES, AND A WORLD OF KNOWLEDGE! 154

INTRODUCTION

CHALLENGING A GIANT!

To take on the matter of the Bible versus Evolution, and to prove the latter as false, is like facing a dragon-like phantasm, a situation in which everything seems vague and uncertain. The debate on whether creationism or evolution is correct just goes on and on and it seems as if no final answer is possible, while even those who stand by the Bible for scientific reasons, often doubt much of what is written in it, and it seems as if the false teachings of evolution are gaining ground on the playing field.

To arrive at truth and break through this barrier of ignorance, we will have to think beyond the obvious, which is the first reason why this book was written. The major reason, though, is that it conveys truth in a pure form, showing not only that the teachings of science and the Bible are completely in line with each other, but also that evolution is false. As the famous mathematician ***Archimedes*** is known for saying: "Give me a long enough lever and a place to stand, and I will move the earth." By using a long and sufficiently strong lever any weight can indeed be moved. The question is: is there such a fixed or reliable foothold from whence evolution can be shaken and proven wrong?

Most people will immediately say "No!" Besides the level of difficulty involved, the world of knowledge is falling apart. As far as truth is concerned, each person, according to his or her own viewpoint, simply quotes from a personal collection of ***learned*** writers or researchers to underscore his or her own beliefs.

Moreover, **modern man** does not enjoy or allow anyone prescribing to him what he should believe! People merely believe what appeals to, or suits them, and most have already decided for themselves what to accept as truth. In this case, that evolution is true, or cannot be reconciled with the Bible.

The Bible, though, is the true Word of God, and we are about to attest to this! After the publication of my earlier books 'The Logos Code' and 'Die Logos Liefdeskode', I felt that many scientific facts relating to the teachings of the Bible which are counter to the theory of evolution, have been omitted or insufficiently discussed in these books and should be brought together in a new volume. Although I would also love to convince sceptics, this book was actually written for believers, with a view to bringing about a more unwavering faith in God. I therefore invite you to accompany me on a journey through science and the Bible.

Some aspects of the book, such as physics, a discussion of atoms, etc., may not interest you and you may think that you will find it boring. Try to persevere though, for, although some sections do not make for easy reading, in the end, it will prove worthwhile. Should you decide not to continue further, you actually place yourself in the position of not being able to comment further concerning evolution and the Bible, and this is a question that simply has to be considered. In the light of the seeming impossibility of reconciling the Bible with science, it may also seem as if God has given us no final answers, but this is not true. Though the Bible doesn't speak the language of science, it indeed provides comprehensive answers to that which He wants us to know; if we would only listen carefully!

God won't give us more answers because his Word is clear enough and committed believers have always heard and understood sufficiently to find peace of mind and to adore Him.

When the rich man mentioned in the Bible asked God to have a messenger sent to his brothers to warn them timeously so that they would not meet eternal doom as he did, God said: "They have Moses and the prophets; let them hear them. If they hear not them, neither will they be persuaded, though one rose from the dead" (Luke, 16:29-31). The recorded words of ***Moses and the prophets*** was the written revelation of God at that time.

In his Word, especially as revealed by Jesus as the 'Word that was made flesh' (cf. John, 1:14, Hebrews, 1:1), God has given us the whole truth, and, as will be seen, Jesus and his wonders mirror and encompass the entire field of science; if only we would have eyes to see and ears to listen!

How important is science? No-one should underrate its value. In line with God's command to, "subdue the earth, and have dominion over every living thing upon the earth" (Genesis 1:28), science investigates our complex world, subjugates it and renders it serviceable to man. From agriculture, which allows us to put food on our tables, to training, housing, health, electronics, etc., science renders a most wonderful service. Because many scientists are also believers, our case is not that of the Bible versus science, but one of truth as opposed to deception, that which causes people to miss the love of God!

Some answers given in this book may indeed sound unusual, because facts are considered that are normally overlooked, and thus may leave one with the feeling that they are merely opinions or philosophies. To an extent this book does encompass new ways of thinking, but you will, however, find that it is fully based on truth, understandable and acceptable.

"Hear thou, then, and be wise" (cf. Proverbs 23:19). Eventually you will find that **science corresponds perfectly with the Bible, while the truth of the Bible, again, is underscored,** because it exactly corresponds with that which can be proven in science. With the same God creating all things, as described by both science and the Bible, what else could we expect? They both relate to the same real world which we live in, and thus simply have to match up. When given all the details, Genesis included, seriously, we indeed find that science walks hand-in-hand with both the Bible and reality as we know it.

Our first question is therefore **why** it is **that science and the Bible seemingly contradict each other?** As we shall see, it is the result of **one crucial fact that is overlooked** in the discussion.

1. ONE FACT CHANGES ALL!

A single fact that is not taken into account can completely disrupt one's outlook on life and have tragic results. Many a child or spouse has indeed already been shot when mistaken for a burglar, and the Titanic sank because, although warned, the crew ignored the fact that they may hit an iceberg. It is estimated that preventable medical errors are the **sixth biggest killer** in America. There are multiple examples of the tragic results of such oversights.

So although it may sound over oversimplified, **one** single fact re-arranges all the arguments on science, evolution and the Bible; the fact that man has fallen into **sin** and we are, due to that, living in a creation under God's curse! (cf. Genesis 3:17).

In all of which follows you will see how determinative this one fact is.

Those who partake of this discussion mostly assume creation as it is now, to be as originally created by God, or as it came into being and developed via the Big Bang, evolution, etc., whilst neither is true. **God's original creation cannot be seen, as it no longer exists!** All of existence was changed by His words: "Cursed is the ground for thy sake" (Genesis

3:17). If we had seen the original, we would have been able to compare it with the present situation, and would clearly have seen that what we now observe is neither what God created, nor the result of evolution and development.

What we now research is a mutilated and defaced reality, far from its original glory. And whilst this is undeniably true, the chemical constitution of what now exists, could not have developed by means of biological processes, but is rather the result of a descent into a state of corruption!

We will need to look deeper in order to better understand this. To treat the present creation as the original is a slap in God's face, as this suggests first that all the decay, agony and death is **His** fault, and second, that murderers, rapists, torturers and even we, in spite of our sins, are all blameless, as this is how we were created.

It is conspicuous how often in the dispute on the supposed difference between the findings of science and Biblical truths that antagonists refer to the case of ***Galileo Galilei***, who declared that the earth rotates around the sun and was subsequently expelled from the church for contradicting its teachings. It is said that, as a result, the church began persecuting scientists and thus created a lasting animosity between church and science. To some extent this statement indeed holds true. All along, however, scientists, evolutionists as well as theologians, in believing that they are still dealing with the original creation, have **erred even more greatly**, with a far worse outcome. This one belief has resulted in all arguments concerning man's origin to be based on false premises, resulting in the erection of houses (theories) of straw!

To grasp the fact that the world which we see is not the original, is a moment of truth. In acknowledging the curse placed on sin, it follows that it can in no way be said that the present state of affairs was brought along by evolution, simply because it is rather a ***DEVOLUTION*** to a now-broken state of affairs, brought about by a single disaster. What we now regard as reality did therefore **not** result from a ***step-by-step*** development! What was perfect became totally changed, defying all ideas of self-development for the better.

If the present state of affairs is not as originally created, how can anyone say that it has been shaped by evolution? If you do not know that a woman was involved in a severe accident, have not seen her beauty prior to it, and how tragedy and surgery completely changed her features, you can neither deduce what she was like before, nor say that her body and face had, in any natural way, developed to her present state!

All deductions ascribing human development to changes in genetic codes (mutations) or hereditary trends simply become laughable and result in false conclusions. With the present situation not being that which God created, the claim that everything evolved from a single point and developed into better and more improved forms, is thus merely hollow reasoning. Not only did matters not improve, but all of existence was also shattered and sent haywire by one event, resulting in a situation in which development was impossible.

Some people will surely deny man's fall into sin. In doing so, however, they not only contradict many verses from Scripture, but cannot give any explanation for the imperfection seen in man and the world. Such a denial will also completely annul the message of the rest of the

Bible, for we clearly read: "**by one man** sin entered into the world, and death by sin; and so death passed upon all men, for that all have sinned" (Romans 5:12). Moreover, if man had not fallen, the statements concerning Jesus becoming man, dying for us, as well as the rest of the New Testament message, all become invalid. If sin does not exist, no-one actually needs either God or salvation.

While no true Bible believer will deny man's sin, it is actually sad that also believers ponder on our origin and evolution without considering God's curse. Important as it is, it is mostly not even mentioned. That science does not busy itself with the matter of sin is understandable, for this is not seen as its task. The reason why theologians overlook it though, is probably just due to the fact that we have not seen the original creation and therefore cannot fathom the change brought to it by God's curse. Also, believers then tend to think that God created everything in terms of substance and atoms, (still to be discussed), while He did not.

This oversight is also possibly due to the fact that either the Bible or science is believed to be erroneous. This relates back to scientific deductions about the present state of creation (discussed under "radiometric tests"), which suggest that that the earth is very ancient, creating the opportunity for evolution and development to have occurred over a long period of time. This contradicts the Biblical narrative of creation taking place in six days, with those supporting the Bible stating that science has to be incorrect, as the Bible is the word of God. This whole debate thus hinges on the acknowledgement of sin.

When we consider the results of sin, we see how closely **scientific** findings actually **correspond to the Bible**, as well as the fact that

evolution itself **cannot be true!** Let's then consider the evidence which proves that what we presently are, and our experience of the world, differs from the original creation, and that **no** conclusions concerning our origin or the doctrine of evolution can be derived from it. You are invited to examine these truths for yourself.

COLLAPSE OF GLORY!

To hear that what we see is not the original creation, but 'collapsed glory' may be just as traumatic as meeting a strange woman and being told that she is your mother, and not the one who raised you and whom you love. Note also, that what we see is not man's true being. In its original pristine state the entire universe was different, created to glorify God, whose glory is above the earth and heaven" (Psalms 148:13), but it has become depraved! What we now see, is broken glory, while our true mother earth was much more beautiful!

Can we prove it? Yes, we are going to provide proof from **all** sides. Still, however, science maintains that there actually is no such thing as final proof. Scientists merely allow reality to speak for itself. When experiments and observation provide overwhelming evidence though, science accepts it as truth until proven wrong. The problem is that the truths accepted by science are also accepted by us, while, in overlooking some points, both theology and science can still be in error.

In the case of man's fall into sin, however, we have overwhelming evidence that God's Word holds true. A true believer would never even dare consider that the God of love and heavenly perfection could have created corrupt, evil things. He could **only** have created **perfection**. We read that after each day of creation He boldly said "It is good," using a

Hebrew word that can also be translated as **'beautiful', 'fine', 'sweet'** or **'well-favoured'.**

The Bible then goes on to tell us why life has become pest- ridden, and everything that is not good can thus only be ascribed to this. His words to Adam after his sin were: "Cursed is the ground for thy sake; in sorrow shalt thou eat of it all the days of thy life; Thorns also and thistles shall it bring forth to thee; and thou shalt eat the herb of the field; In the sweat of thy face shalt thou eat bread, till thou return unto the ground; for out of it wast thou taken: for dust thou art, and unto dust shalt thou return" (Genesis 3:17-19)."

Considering the profound consequences of sin, what happened to the "ground" is indeed a metaphor for our present existence! Note the words; "for thy sake", whereby God directly ascribes all imperfection to man's sin. Since He created life as perfect, where does brokenness and suffering then come from **if not** from the curse on **sin?** With the consequences of sin being so evident, how can His words not be true? The Bible provides the only real answer to all of life's agonies.

"Cursed," means that He, as punishment, brought about a ***changed dispensation*** which encompassed all of existence, as experienced daily in our 'broken' world and reality. Man now had to sweat in order to produce his food, often with little or no success. The idea of spontaneous development and improvement as proposed by the theory of evolution cannot account for man's present travail. In terms of this theory, he should have been better off than his animal ancestors.

Now it seems that the animal-kingdom does the least work to get food, while it is man who sinned, that suffers most. Unfortunately, the fact that animals also suffer just further proves that we are now living on cursed ground. Paul aptly describes the collapse of glory saying: "The whole creation groaneth and travaileth in pain together; not only they, but ourselves also... groan within ourselves..." under the agony caused by sin (cf. Romans 8:20-23). God further portrays the decay that has crept into the lives of both man and nature by saying, "I had planted thee a noble vine, wholly a right seed... thou turned into the degenerate plant of a strange vine (Jerimiah 2:21).

Also note that the **same** corruption took place within man's **spirit**, in which the consequences of sin are even more apparent. Paul's exposition; "all have sinned and come short of the glory of God" (Romans 3:23), shows that the corruption extends down into man's heart: "all men are gone out of the way... are become unprofitable; there is none that doeth good. Their throat is an open sepulcher; with their tongues they deceive; the poison of asps is under their lips: Their mouth full of cursing and bitterness, their feet swift to shed blood: Destruction and misery are in their ways: And the way of peace have they not known: There is no fear of God before their eyes. Now we know that... the entire world is guilty before God" (cf. Romans 3:12-19).

This also brings us to the idea of ***spiritual death***. Because Adam still lived for 900 years before he actually died, God's promise that should they eat from the forbidden tree they would **die that day** (cf. Genesis 2:17), rather points to a 'spiritual' death. In other words, Adam became dead unto Him, missing true life as He created it. Man's **soul** had become dead unto God; dead in sin and desperately in need of salvation. Beatific life itself had died, and if man does not regain this life by 'rebirth', he will, alas, eternally experience a living death: painfully dying while still living (cf. Ephesians 2:1-6; Daniel 12:2).

Sin further brought **'nakedness'** to man; the feeling of being uncovered, exposed and appalling, which we can very well understand, as we certainly won't go shopping naked without feeling horrible humiliation. Man's original carefree happiness was described by one simple word; "***unashamed***"; a happy beauty, devoid of shame (cf. Genesis 2:25). After sinning, though, they are described as naked, and went and hid because of becoming painfully aware of this nakedness. They made themselves aprons from fig leaves, as seeing themselves naked was embarrassing to them.

This was also the beginning of the **big *cover-up***; clothes, cosmetics, soap and deodorants! As they were naked before the fall but not ashamed, we sense that this new awareness of nakedness, accompanied by fear, actually has deep meaning. Before, they had felt amiably innocent, but now nakedness was experienced as a feeling of both spiritual and moral disgrace.

Within their very hearts they experienced despicable ugliness; not good to behold; the repulsiveness of broken beauty. They had lost the glory of the image of God (cf. Romans 3:23).

While sweating is part of the curse and loss of glory, they would from then on know what it is to be smelly and unattractive, to get tired, feel pain, be hurt and to bleed. Sweat glands as well as unsightly hair growth, fangs, nails and claws, weeds and thorny bushes all became part of a new, unpleasant reality (cf. Genesis 3:18,19). The once glorious splendor had become hostile; anguish and fear of death now permeated life as a whole. Droughts and pests would eat away at their harvests and rain cause floods (cf. Psalms 77:18). Besides sweat glands, vast bodily changes, including the forming of intestines enabling digestion and bodily excretions, clearly took place.

While all unpleasant things originate from the fall, man surely did not have to deal with this before. In their exalted state food must have been **fully absorbed** by their bodies, as in the case when the angels ate with Abraham, or Jesus with his disciples after his resurrection (as we will later see, this is because any form of energy can be converted back to pure energy). Angels and people in heaven indeed also eat. Cf. Psalm 78:25: "bread of angels"; Matthew 8:11, the feast in heaven, and 26:29: 'I will not drink henceforth of this fruit of the vine, until that day when I drink it new with you in my Father's kingdom." As is the case with heaven, Eden had no toilets.

Broken glory furthermore brought **disharmony** between Adam and his wife. They blamed each other (cf. Genesis 3:12, 13). Their loving relationship with God was also shattered. Instead of feelings of enthusiastic love, animosity and fear had now entered; "I heard your voice and was afraid because I was naked." They went and hid. With the new fearsome feeling of vulnerability, life as a whole had lost its glory. Don't we all know this inclination to shun away from God? Man's own heart, with its feelings of guilt, its predisposition to hate and to fear, is exhibit A in the case which proves the Bible to be true.

The ***thorns and thistles*** mentioned represent all hurting aspects of life. It was not a total change, food is still available, but it has become perishable. Beauty still abounds, and in magnitude and design, still glorify God. Yet, in this cursed state, everything began to malfunction. The cruelty of the food chain was initiated, animal living off animal. Yet, in the beginning all animals had been given green plants as food (cf. Genesis 1:29-30).

So did **suffering** enter; decay, hunger, war, sorrow, feelings of insecurity, mutilation by murder..., and eventually all beauty ending with a tombstone! We are living under the shadow of death, and all of our trials and tribulations prove God's words to be true. Nothing that caused hurt or death was part of original, exalted creation, which was aimed at pure bliss. Before the fall, disease was surely unknown. Afterwards, micro-organisms that could transform into evil germs and viruses came into existence, resulting in malady and decay. Even poison could not have been part of the original reality. Food was easy to get and even spiders did not kill other insects. Since the curse, however, everything has become hateful. Like thorns, mechanisms for attack and defense such as fangs, some carrying venom, could only have resulted from the curse! Now, toxic plants, spiders and snakes threaten life, whilst droughts, typhoons and floods take food from the table. Every facet of life carries the potential for disaster, and each cell in our bodies can turn malignant. Everything has now become hard and dreadful, as opposed to the original life, which was perfect and coveted.

All this points to the **drastic change** sin has brought to the human genetic-code, which will be discussed later; and this includes transformations to man's spirit! Hereditary diseases in ***innocent*** babies are deadly proof that evil, and the curse on sin, are carried over to succeeding generations. Domino blocks, when set up, all fall in sequence when the first one goes. Adam's fall was "passed upon all men, for all have sinned" (Romans 5:12). From conception, all are laden with guilt (cf. Psalms 51:5). The kernel and process of life was damaged. Every tear in our world proves it. God also added that man will return to dust, appointing death as the only departure from this world of suffering.

Sin has thus clothed all the beautiful properties of the original creation in '***collapsed glory***', corruption and ruin. (Original Greek: mataiotēs: meaning transient or temporary, and phthora: to decay or to perish (cf. Romans 8:20-21). The words; "the creature was made subject to vanity" (was subjected to transience), implies that it was not like this from the beginning!

The very basis of life has been ruined, subjected to decay. Anyone who denies this will have to prove it wrong and show where else the anguish in life could possibly have originated!

If we suppose that ***spontaneous development*** (evolution) could indeed explain our origin, why then did everything not develop even more perfectly in all aspects? Where did the germ of evil sneak in to cause such misery? Also, germs and viruses have specific **chemical** compositions aimed at destroying life. If life originated from chemical reactions, what has entered since these reactions so as to shape pain and hatred in man's **heart**? Evolution must then be the ***father of torment*** by introducing it into an otherwise beautiful system, with suffering as its offspring. Evolution as a process is thus not fascinating at all!

According to evolution, beings and processes always improve, but now life is getting harder. Society now more represents the ***survival of the vilest*** rather than of the ***fittest!*** If everything has developed for the better, why then do we now still experience the worst brutality, crime, diseases and disfigurement among human beings, which are supposed to be the **highest** form of life?

This reveals a serious flaw in evolution's high-minded theory, which reasons that chemicals can by themselves, decide to develop and reach even greater heights. Evolutionism credits an ***almighty intelligence*** to atoms and cells in improving themselves and progressing, presenting beautifully-sounding concepts such as dynamic autopoiesis (dynamic self-doing), or "developmental and self-organizing systems". Not even man as the highest-developed being can produce new body parts as he wishes, cause parts that have been lost to grow back, or even prevent disease! Brainless molecules cannot decide what they are, wish to be, or are going to do!

If we don't consider God's curse, how could everything then have developed into such intricate complexity and yet contain all the facets of wickedness that can produce the worst in man and in the end usually do? The **only** reason why evolutionists cannot explain why things are simultaneously so wondrous and still subject to decay, is that the results of **sin** are not considered.

Furthermore, the term 'self-development' is unscientific, because science only operates on the principle (logic) of cause and effect, and apart from having a separate creator, no logical cause for our existence can be given.

Even self-declared atheists like Aldous Huxley later confessed that he simply did not want to acknowledge God, for, if he did, he could no longer do what he wished without feeling guilty. Rejecting Him (God) is just an escape route.

The fact that only the Bible provides an explanation for our broken world, (which evolution does not), just points to the credibility of the Bible. The present harsh consequences of sin correspond perfectly with what God said would happen should man disobey. Our suffering proves Him to be real and alive, for his words precisely and painfully take shape in our reality (cf. Genesis 3:16-19). Moreover, while his Word remains true, nothing is said in the Bible of a continuous development from simple to more complex life-forms, rather the evidence points to everything being at first perfect, and then **abruptly entering into corruption!**

2. SCIENCE, ENERGY AND... ATOMS!

In the light of this evidence, Adam could **not** have been created as we now know man to be; immoral and subject to death. He was NOT like us, for he was created GOOD and PERFECT. To get an idea of the initial creation, we will have to take a good look at how things are now, first, as described by science, and then compare this to what the Bible says about man's state **before** his fall. Again, you will simply have to consider this argument before you will be able to partake of any further discussion on evolution. This argument actually **proves the Bible to be true, because it concurs with the present views of science. Likewise, you can accept science as true, because it is supported by the Bible.**

The similarity between the teachings of the Bible and science becomes more striking when we consider **energy**. Science tells us that everything consists of, or is, energy. To many this may sound impossible, for to our minds energy just is some obscure ***power***. It just is a fact, though, that everything **consists of** energy, just emerging in different forms. Wood, light, heat, sound, rock, our bodies, etc.; whatever we see, touch or call matter (or material), is just energy in different forms. Though it can present itself as a tangible substance, such as water as ice, snow or steam, everything just is energy and can be converted into other forms, For example, during burning, the potential energy in wood and the chemicals on the head of a match is converted into ashes, smoke and light and heat energy. It is still the **same** energy, but has changed in form. In the end energy (from the Greek word 'energeia'), is not just an aspect of life, but its building blocks. Scientists define energy as **that** active principle ***which makes work possible***. As it transforms, it has the ability to activate other things. For example, gasoline is a substance and yet also a driving force, and all matter operates in the same way. "Every gram of iron, sand, and so on, contains enough energy to make 200 000 tons of water boil; one cubic meter of sea-water contains enough energy to boil the water in all oceans" (R. Feynman; Nobel Prize winner in physics).

Let's begin with the **sun**. All of earthly life is sustained by energy from the sun, which radiates massive amounts of it by the burning of its constituent elements. Through the electro-magnetic radiation of light and ultra-violet rays the sun not only supplies us with heat energy so that we won't freeze, but it is also converted into many other forms. Plants convert the light into chemical energy and store it as starches, sugars, etc., in their cells. We eat plants as an energy-supply to make our bodies function, as food consists of energy and also provides it. Energy stored by plants, is the energy found in so-called "***fossil*** fuels" like petroleum, coal, and gas. We convert the energy in these fuels into other forms for own use. In power plants, coal is burnt to convert chemical energy into electrical energy (electricity), and we burn wood or use this electricity for heat and to cook food. In engines, gasoline made from coal is burnt in order to convert this chemical energy into kinetic energy to drive motors, trains and other modes of transport. When you boil water for coffee, you are just converting electric energy into heat energy, or when cooking over an open fire, the energy in the wood is converted into heat. In this way **energy is continuously converted into other forms while in the process nothing is lost.** We sit, walk and sleep on energy. It enables us to work and our minds to think. Even in thinking about it now, we are expending energy. It is the underlying substance and driving-force of all matter.

WHAT IS THE POINT?

What is important is that energy itself has changed, and thus none of existence is still as it was in the beginning. What God created was perfect and had it stayed that way, decay, rotting, death, pain, stench and feelings of shame, would not have occurred. These were **not** part of the original creation. This means that, as we will later and more adequately reveal, energy must, in very important ways, have **differed** from that which it is now, able to work without embodying the results of the curse. ***Thorns*** signify the ability to cause pain, to hurt and to be felt by man. Note that the appearance of thorns on plants implies a physical change in their chemistry and DNA; and so do sweat glands. This means that **atomic structures** having a composition that can decay, be damaged and rot, including our physical bodies, which can be injured and die, all **result from the fall.**

Situations like poisoning and disease involve definite physical changes in chemical compositions in the body of the afflicted person. As I said, a similar change took place in man's **spirit** and there are now multiple 'spiritual' diseases which include feelings of guilt, anxiety, loneliness and others that were not part of the original creation. Man's fall brought about a ***'collapse of glory'*** affecting the full spectrum of life, distorting radiant beauty into grotesque forms, bringing about all kinds of depravity, as well as the atomic decay as revealed in the Laws of Thermodynamics that we will discuss later.

Considering all of this in the light of the heavenly life in the original perfect creation of God, leads us to conclude that the curse uttered upon the earth brought about an immense change, resulting in what we **now** know as the ***sub-atomic*** **world** of harsh matter!

When we then read that Adam was created from the ***dust*** of the earth (cf. Genesis 2:7), we can, in the light of the above, take it to mean that it was **not** the particle-matter as it now exists. It was an unblemished, un-cursed creation. Only after Adam's fall do we hear of the negative consequences encompassing all of creation. The original creation was **not** composed of solid particles as it now is. This means that also the present chemical constitution of things as elements and atoms results from man's fall. Although this change is hard to describe, we all now experience it. We will return later to examine what it must have been like in the beginning.

Let us clearly state that, although it is not the role of science to provide answers on why death and decay have become part of our everyday lives, those who attempt to base the theory of evolution on a scientific knowledge of chemicals and developmental processes, may just as well forget it. I stress it again, if everything had developed by means of a process of evolution, reaching such heights of beauty so as to form a rose, a hummingbird, man's amazing brain and so on, where and how did death and corruption seep in so as to cause so much agony? In no way can evolution explain suffering and death.

If we accept the fact of man's fall, it is clear that if man was, according to evolution, the last living being to arrive on the scene, and death only results from **his** sin, with millions of years passing before his arrival, **there would have been no fossil record of animals that had died before man. Moreover, if they were also not subject to the curse as stated in Romans, chapter 8, the animals that lived before the earth was cursed would still be alive.**

This means that all of the fancy terminology, names, technical and biological data used by evolutionists in their arguments is totally meaningless ... for what we now see is built upon the changes brought about by the curse!

BEHOLD THE END!

The fact that the universe as energy in the form of chemical compositions cannot be what God originally created, can also be seen in the promises of how life will be again after He restores it to glory. All at once the elements will burn and disappear (dissolve), indicating that the realm introduced by sin has passed. On "the day of the Lord... the heavens shall pass away with a great noise, the elements shall melt with fervent heat, the earth also ... shall be burned up. We look for new heavens and a new earth, wherein dwelleth righteousness" (cf. 2 Peter 3:3-13).

The Bible does not say that the old heavens and earth will be annulled or be replaced by something else; rather that it will be made new. The Greek word "kainos," as in: "I make all things new"

(Revelations 21:5), does not mean the same as "neos," (new, as in 'it has not existed before''), but rather, "new in character"; a **marvellously fresh existence!** What had become corrupted will be "changed" in the same way as believers' bodies will be changed into bodies of glory (cf. Hebrews 1:12, 1 Corinthians 15:50, 53), thus a ***restoration*** of the original creation in which the "moth and rust" that corrupts will not exist (cf. Matthew 6:20), and not a totally new creation.

Man will again be as he ***was meant to be***. Jesus said, "When they shall rise from the dead... they are as the angels which are in heaven" (Mark 12:25, Matthew 22:30). The children of God will thus again have spiritual bodies and an untainted existence as originally created by God, and no longer be a cluster of enfolding atoms that can lose electrons, decay and age. As will be seen later, there could indeed have been a difference in love-energy between the constituents of original man and angels, for we read in the Bible, "Thou madest **him a little lower than the angels**; thou crownedst him with glory and honour, and didst set him over the works of thy hands" (Hebrews 2:7). Man's original make-up was therefore **not** as we are now.

This also means that when He makes everything new, energy/ matter as we know it will be **changed back to pure love-energy**, so as to bring about perfectly new heavens and earth. Nothing will be destroyed; just be made gloriously new. Nothing God has created will just vanish. Either in heavenly light or the darkness of damnation, it will continue forever. All energy in the cosmos will just be transformed into a new and perfect state! Peter calls it: "the day in which the heavens shall pass away with a great noise and the elements shall melt with fervent heat" (cf. 2 Peter 3:10-13). All will be engulfed in a single celestial level of energy! Glory will be returned to a wonderland of sparkling beauty. The curse will be removed and earth renewed to a paradisiacal state (cf. Isaiah 65:17–25).

3. LOVE AS ARCHITECT!

While it is above dispute that man's fall into sin has brought about a vast change in creation, the original state of perfect energy could not have been as it now is. In all that has been said so far, we repeatedly conjure up ***flashes of the glory*** of what life could and should have been. What then was the nature of the original creation? We will return to the scientific evidence later, but in answering this question, we see a most sublime picture unfolding. The fact that God, who "**IS** Love," is **also the Creator** (1 John 4:8), means that the universe was designed and created BY Love to BE love; all consisting of different nuances of love-energy. As He is love, could creation, both in the being of man and visible reality have been anything else? No! The total make-up of life was love, and it is the changes brought about by sin that now causes it to be an imperfect reflection of Him!

So as to fully grasp the idea that everything could have consisted of love, first consider the fact that **love is more** than just a ***feeling***. To many people love may sound like sissy-talk. A vital question is thus what love actually is and what the statement "God is love" really means. If it is just a feeling, is God also just a feeling, dreamlike and vulnerable?

Surely not! "Strong" as in, "Love is strong as death" (Songs 8:6), signifies something passionate and powerful, while the words "as death" imply that love has devastating power; fearlessly faces and conquers all that oppose it; can build or demolish; cross oceans or oppose and even conquer death, in the same way that when death calls, not even the strongest can resist it. To see the truth of it, just try to take a baby elephant or gorilla from its mother or harm a man's bride, and see how furious and strong ***love*** can be.

Such is God, who can give life or take it back. Solomon continues, "The coals thereof are coals of fire... a most vehement flame." The statement that ***God is love*** shows that love is none other than the **most concrete mode of existence, *the perfect way of being,*** from which everything flows. It implies infinitely more than mere feelings, and is the actual outpouring of a person's being; in God's case, Almighty Being. Although we may find it strange that an attribute such as love which is **invisible**, could have created the world, **God** Himself is **not invisible**. Once we "shall see Him (Love) as He is" (cf. 1 John 3:2); Almighty God!

To grasp how all of creation could consist of love in a spiritual form, it is also important to understand that our normal concept of ***'spiritual'*** is one of weakness and being inferior to what is ***physical***. It is just the other way round. Physics, (or physical) from the Greek word "phusis", depicts **the working or dynamics of energy**, and does not refer to strength versus feebleness, which is exactly how science uses the word. And God as Creator, being able to sustain all of existence, would therefore have to be most "***physical***" being possible and the pinnacle of physics, the working Power in and behind the entire universe. "Physics" then is merely our scientific way of describing how He makes things work in our sphere. We only see physics as differing from the spiritual because of the corruption in thinking that sin has introduced, resulting in our adopted the erroneous idea of "spiritual" as weakness. Yes, our perception of physical as referring to **rigid** structures or harsh acts also stems from the changes brought about by the curse, while, as we will later see, God's ***spiritual*** workings can also be regarded as **physical**.

Note that **none** of the powers He instituted to form, shape and sustain the universe consist of matter, but are **invisible forces** which can only be detected by what they do. For example, **fire**, which has no firm or fixed body, is still substance, having a **dreadful power** that can liquefy the strongest steel. This is also the case with **gravity**, which is powerful enough to keep massive heavenly bodies in orbit, yet is intangible and does not have a basis in atoms. The force of gravity represents immense physical power. This is also the case with light rays, weak and strong atomic bonds, magnetism and centrifugal forces, which are all invisible and without form, yet represent terrifyingly powerful bonds of love (attraction), keeping our bodies intact and planets and stars and on their fixed trajectories in space. Love, which instituted all these forces so as to order and make life and the cosmos possible, can therefore in no way be considered a fleeting feeling, but is God's almighty potency of doing whatever He wishes.

This also relates to our bodies. That we are flesh and blood does not mean that man was originally like this, or even that it differs that much from the heavenly state. On heaven's spiritual level peoples' ***spiritual*** bodies can surely be seen with **physical** (real) eyes (cf. Revelations 20:12); which would still have been the case had sin not corrupted God's physics! We may also add that we are already now spiritual beings, but not as we tend to understand it, as differing from the physical.

Also consider that we tend to see love just as an emotion or feeling."Emotion" as a word, though, is derived from "emovere" (Latin), where e- (a variant of ex-), means "out," and "movere: means "to move"; or the movement in and "flowing out from" one; which is energy! Dictionaries describe emotions as "mental states accompanied by feelings and behavior." While God IS love and almighty Creator, to say that emotion is just a state or feeling, can neither be a sufficient nor correct description. He is living Love upholding creation. Although love also exists between people, the Bible does not call love an emotion, but just treats it as a reality; in this case, as a **person** (God), whose entire personality is described as, "Love." This also is true about people: when you are **mad**, **you** become madness, when you hate, **you** are hatred. Paul also personifies love by saying: "love is kind, is not puffed up....." (cf. 1 Corinthians 13:4,5) and talks about love as if it is a liquid substance, "shed abroad in hearts by the Holy Ghost" (from the Greek "ekcheõ", to "pour out") (Romans 5:5). Note that both love and hate changes the whole person and becomes visible in certain actions, in the case of hate, causing war and madness, in the case of love, bliss. **Emotion is thus the strongest driving force in the universe**, and when Paul writes; "Nothing shall be able to separate us from the love of God, which is in Christ Jesus our Lord" (Romans 8:39), he means that the love protecting us is stronger than all other thinkable powers! Love is.... strong!

In the same way that flames are fire's mode of expression, saying that God is love is not describing some feeling, but rather describing the brilliance of God. As the perfect Being, He does not just express love to an extent, but his very Being **is** love. And as a diamond's glitter cannot be separated from itself, but is the very expression of the diamond, so IS God also the very love that He expresses. Love is thus not **one** of his many attributes; He **IS** indestructible Love! What moves in Him, is love in all of its aspects and qualities. It is emitted from Him, moving all of heavenly life and the universe according to his will; as effortless as the sun and water droplets create a rainbow. Surely, love includes all the nuances of activity, for He is also supremely happy and merciful (cf. 1 Timothy 6:15; Psalm 103:8), and all his attributes just are **facets** or **shades** of Love's beaming face, like the colors of a rainbow which together form white light. Even when He righteously punishes, it is because his love cannot stand anything opposing Him.

This means that emotion is not a mere addition to life. As created BY Love, it still IS emotion, but as a result of the curse on sin, love in all earthly nuances has become blemished and harsh. While creation is a radiant expression of love, shaping all forms, the only reason why we don't see it in this way, is the "collapse of glory" brought about by the curse on sin (cf. Genesis 3:17).

Because our existence is seen as tough and sometimes even unpleasant, it **appears** to completely differ from love, causing us to think that this harsh and rigid life could never have been created by a power called Love, and which IS love. Love is now often viewed as secondary and powerless, whilst it is not! As mentioned, unblemished life, light and sound in heaven impossibly consist of atomic parts like photons or be carried by sound-waves, while in the perfect state of heaven they, as light and sound, just is the same. Angels' bodies, unlike ours, are also spiritual, for they indeed are spirits (cf. Hebrews 1:14), yet they are **more solid and stronger** than anything we know. **Not even a nuclear bomb can harm them**, precisely because the spiritual realm is exalted above atomic structures and fission.

Also consider that, after the renewal of the heavens and earth, resurrected bodies in glorified form will be real, permanent and visible. What can actually be said about the present solidity of our world? As a result of the fall, everything now corrodes, dies or can disintegrate to form mere gaseous clouds. Love, though, is **more substantial than anything else** and never fails (cf. 1 Corinthians 13:8; NIV).

To behold creation as Love-energy will surely astound us and introduce a completely new way of thinking. Allow truth to dawn, however; as it can be none other! Anyone who differs from this explanation will first have to more adequately explain exactly what ***love*** is, why Love is the **Creator**, and why one mere smile of true love can change hearts, (physical) facial expressions and actions; and even prevent fighting and war! More will be said of this later. Everything, man included, initially consisted of pure e-motive (out-moving) love-energy exuded by the God of love, **only becoming hardened structures composed of atoms, now experienced as uncertain and brutal, after man's fall.** The curse on sin distorted all of creation, transforming it from radiant beauty to rigidity, from eternal life to being subject to decay. Now a broken beauty, which leads us to conclude that the actual **sub-atomic world** of particles, was **brought about by the curse** uttered over earth. This instituted a phenomenal change, materializing glory into the harshness, decay and death we now know. As already stated, prior to the curse, atoms as such did not exist; shades of love-energy merely displayed God's attributes so as to make Him known as pure love. Now, however, what love has become, hurts and scuffs our bodies and feelings. The same hardening that entered man's heart has spoilt all of creation (cf. Isaiah 6:6, Mark 6:52)!

Exactly what is included in this "harshness" brought about by sin is difficult to describe. It did not introduce a physical reality in place of a spiritual reality, because, as I said, in "LOVE" everything has the same powerful spiritual essence. The difference is therefore between a perfect, unblemished reality and a loss of this perfection, causing it to **appear** as if physical things are something **other** than spiritual! Because we have never seen this perfect state, we can only envision it by thinking of angels and Jesus Himself, who, after his resurrection, could transcendently pass through walls. We will not be able to aptly describe it and no comparison will actually do. We cannot, for example, compare the original creation to a baby's skin that later becomes hard and wrinkled, a rose scorched by fire, food that becomes putrefied, metals that rust and so on, for these are the **same** baby, food or metal which now simply consists of corrupted energy. This all takes place at the level of an already fallen state, and therefore cannot indicate what the original state was like.

What the curse brought with it is love distorted into hatefulness and the tendency to become even more corrupted. We could liken it to tender love that turns into hatred when one is rejected. What we now see in both man's body and spirit, is the harsh reality of atoms and emotions such as hatred, fear and so on, as revealed in the symbolism of ***thorns and thistles*** now able to injure life, an all-engulfing change from pure affection to what we now know as chemicals and natural things.

Note that the same can be said about the matter (energy) in both man's body and spirit. Both have become rough, dangerous, hurting and unfriendly, bringing about an undesired hardness and rigidity as well as a sloppiness and messiness which is just as detestable in fallen man as in nature itself. Both now ***fall short of the glory of God***, lacking the benevolence and trustworthiness of perfect love. The collapse of glory thus means that the original creation has fallen into a rigid material form which has resulted in all energy now being detestable and subject to decay, a deviation from the original pristine state.

Also note that hatred is not really the ***opposite*** of love, as if after the fall love continued to exist, man still is able to love and can choose between the two, only being hateful on occasion or to various degrees. The emotion of love, like the rest of the original creation, had become a corrupted, shattered shadow of its former beauty. One may describe a ruined painting as now being 'opposite' to its original state, but strictly speaking, this is not correct. It is the **same** painting, only now it has lost its beauty and become disgraced, and worthless.

The choice against the Will of God as creator brought about the decomposition of the love-energy of which everything consisted, killing the soul. Man now embodied a corrupted form of love and thus became a nuance of darkness. That which he still calls love is actually selfishness or hatred in the guise of love, a selfish love that emerges only when he chooses; a difference that man himself does not even realize, because he has been blinded by sin (cf. Luke 6:41).

Although all of life has become harsh, some people and features of nature such as flowers may still seem perfectly fine and good. Only for a time, though, as everything now deteriorates, rots and eventually dies. A beautiful sunset may be followed by an earthquake, and at times man may pretend to be kindness itself, but under certain circumstances, becomes a monster. We can still appreciate the beauty of a tiger, an anaconda's colorful skin or spiders that mimic flowers to entice insects. So complex is the deformity that these still appear wondrous, but under the right circumstances, they can be devouring horrors.

We may view this situation as ***simply the way things are***, but this is **not** how God created it. Sublime life has become brutal. In short, love-energy has itself become a hateful, offensive and corrupted beauty, with an inherent depravity that, in due course, will become more visible, and this is true for all of creation. As mentioned earlier, according to 1 Corinthians 15: 49-53, the **real difference** that has entered is that what now exists is flesh, blood, corruption and weakness, as opposed to a sublime and incorruptible heavenly state; a harsh transitoriness in place of perfect and everlasting life!

EMANATION!?

To say that ***God is energy*** would be impersonal and stain his glory with our frail conceptualisation of the state. Yet He is the fountain from whence all energy in the cosmos flows. This is not just philosophizing, for, if God **is** love, all of creation in the beginning must also have been ***love***. **Period!** Later we will more closely examine this statement and the scientific evidence to support it, but it can now be said that everything emerged from the power of LOVE, and the all-powerful will of God to do as He wishes.

In the theological world the idea of ***emanation***, that creation is a direct emission flowing from God, meets with strong opposition. Let's think about it again. Surely creation is no ***extension*** of God so that it could be considered as divine. Part of Him did not flow out in the form of creation, nor did He express into creation as if it was Himself. As the Almighty He merely created a new reality in its own right, expressing Himself in a new level of love-energy apart from Him and the heavenly life, sustained by the powers He built into it. Reality today is just a fallen form of that original creation. Consider then, that creation, although distorted by sin, is still nothing other than **his** love that became corrupted; just as man, depraved by sin, still is his creation. His divinity can still be seen in it (cf. Romans 1:19,20). Try as you may, it is simply impossible to show any difference between His attributes and those He displays in His creation. ***Love*** simply is **love**; ***wisdom*** is **wisdom** and ***power***, **power**; there are not two kinds of each. Love, mercy, wisdom and all His other attributes, remain the same whether in Him, expressed by a mother, embodied in the rain, roses or whatever. He is, but He also gives rise to the love, wisdom and other aspects seen in his ability to sustain all, as well as in the good attributes in man, animals and nature. “The earth is full of his mercy” (Psalms 119:64).

Also, consider that, although our existence is of a lower rank than His and the sphere of heaven, we can in no way say that the love and wisdom in Jesus as **God** differs from His pure love as God who became **man**; it is the same! This also helps us to understand His ***two natures***, and the reason why He could seamlessly become God and man, and be perfect in both. The love was the same in both, and as a result, Jesus had no sin.

Surely the distinct properties of God’s nature in Jesus would have been conserved? Even though all of God’s attributes were not fully passed to Him as man (cf. Mark 13:32), God was n**ot diminished** by his humanity. He, as God, was still able, as man, to do whatever He wished without being restricted by his manhood, or experience any loss to His love and wisdom. We should therefore, neither view it as the ***intermingling*** of two natures resulting in a new personality, nor that they were ***divided*** in any way as God and Son of God. God just gave Himself, "in the likeness of sinful flesh," so as to suffer and die for us (Romans 8:3), and Jesus thus perfectly fitted the situation.

Surely, also, only by his **power** as **God**, could He have carried the full load of wrath against all of mankind's sin and in his divine nature experience hunger, suffering and death, while as God, He could not die. Altogether, though, He was and still is love, using and imparting His attributes as He wishes. Because **love just is love**, it is also the same love which He as God and God who became man, pours out into us (cf. Romans 5:5), and as Love, lives within us (cf. Galatians 2:20). This shows also that true love, as it exists in reborn believers, does not differ from Him.

Although He established creation on its own footing, all of existence thus still is, ***of, and through*** him (cf. Romans 11: 36). The reason that we tend to think that His love differs from what we find in creation, only results from the fact that sin has defiled love, it no longer has the appearance of God and is not experienced as such. Pure Love in Him, however, could never have changed.

Apart from the fact that creation is not God Himself, the problem surrounding emanation has more to do with the fact that omnipotence cannot become less or lose quality by an outpouring during the creation of something new. He simply cannot be lessened, whether He creates the cosmos, becomes a seed in a mother, or a baby in a manger. This also underscores the fact that He himself could **not** be affected even when what He had created had become defiled. It is thus **precisely the blemished creation which withholds us from talking about emanation** because we are reluctant to ascribe the depravity we see to God, a reluctance resulting in a loss, as in this way we cut creation loose from its ***foundation*** and are left speechless as to explain its origin and essence.

To return to His beauty, however, the Bible does not say that everything consists of either energy or love; it simply portrays our world as a ***rainbow***, a multi-colored exhibition of glory flowing from the God of love! (cf. ***Ezekiel 1***; Psalms 8:1,5; Romans 1:20). Like a manager's instructions, God's commands are materialized, and creation built and sustained according to his wishes. When the Almighty speaks, his words have the power of creation. His divine energy, as source of power, wisdom and love, gives stature to all beauty. In His omnipotence, He willed all the necessary powers of creation, those we now call nuclear-power, gravitation, magnetism and so on. This does not mean that He ***is* energy** or ***energy is God***; just that it emanates from his power and ability to do whatever He wishes. All powers are merely nuances of His power, given specific attributes as to perform allocated tasks.

Lovers of science will appreciate that, in spite of all our knowledge, we really do not know exactly what electricity or gravity are, only what they do. The fact that all things are, in reality, merely God's energy in action, makes it easier to grasp that Jesus, having power over all, could make use of an ordinary boat, **change** molecular structure so as to produce something else (converting water into wine), **multiply** and grow these structures (the bread and fishes), or simply **ignore** the laws of physics as if they played no part at all, such as the time that He walked on water, and after his resurrection, was able to pass through walls (cf. John 20:19-25).

Omnipotence means that He can do what He likes! By the same power, He could take a part of Adam's side and use it to make a wife, cause Aaron's walking-stick to flower, produce ripe almonds (cf. Numbers 17:8), make the blind to see and so on. He can give life or return it to the dead, as in the case of Lazarus, but can also end life, such as when He cursed the fig-tree and caused it to immediately wither. This is why a star could be seen, not far out in the sky, but right above a stable, to show where He would be born as a man, **created at His command!**

His ability to walk on the sea confused the disciples, "For they considered not the miracle of the loaves: for their heart was hardened" (cf. Mark 6:52). They did not understand that this miracle showed that His power overrules gravity and all other forces in nature. The fact that He could walk on water and create bread from nothing, proves that natural laws and forces such as gravity and the wind, are subject to Him. Metaphysical power is the stronger, but can fuse with natural forces to direct them, such as when He stilled the storm and healed people!

Both Theology and science treat the **same** topic: supernatural life, for **all** has a supernatural basis; physical and metaphysical have a single source in God. He walks on the ***foundation*** of our existence, it is **His power!** There actually is no difference between God and energy/matter. Omnipotence means that He is infinite energy and can apply it as He wishes; Love emanating love! At the time of creation the Word was; and the Word created matter (cf. John 1:3). So the Word presented itself again when He became a man of flesh and blood, ***clothed*** in our fallen matter/energy, to bring forth his love in the stature of His own creation! (cf. John 1:14).

In the end, all the details provided in the Bible, even those sections which some people call mere ***stories***, actually underscore the truth of the Bible. As previously mentioned, science is not to blame for not having all the answers; for it only explores the world we now live in. To focus blindly only on scientific findings, however, will be a grave mistake and take us nowhere.

SCIENTIFIC BACKUP?

It now becomes easier to see how perfectly science and the Bible support each other in portraying **one truth**, merely using **different terms** to describe the **same** phenomena. For instance, the concept "energy", meaning "to work", as science also uses it, is derived from the Greek word "***energeia***," which is often used in the New Testament. We hear, for example, that God shew forth mighty works ("energousin") in Jesus (cf. Matthew 14:2). It is also applied to the motions of sin which ***work*** ("energeō"; Romans 7:5) in our members, and mentioned in the text "there are diversities of gifts of the Spirit but the same God ***worketh*** ("energēma") all in all" (cf. 1 Corinthians 12:6,11). Finally we read that "God ***worketh*** ("energeō") all things after the counsel of his will…." (cf. Ephesians 1:11, Philipians 2:13).

It even applies to the end days, we hear, in which God will change everything, even our vile body, "to be fashioned like unto his glorious body, according to the ***working*** ("energeia") whereby he will subdue all things unto himself" (cf. Philippians 3:21). Paul also says he was made a minister according to the ***working*** ("energeia") of His power (cf. Ephesians 3:7), the same power **by which He upholds all things** (cf. Hebrews 1:3).

This all shows that God's works and activities on **all** levels are forms of love-energy energizing life. Although his work in the cosmos and in men cannot be directly seen, He works ("energeō") in all spheres to uphold life, which is exactly what science seeks to explore. By attributing everything to the activity of ***energy***, science reveals a good understanding of creation. If you believe that God as Creator is active in both creation and people, it does not really matter whether you understand quantum physics or not; his continued activity is a **fact**.

Surely it is not science's task to show us that life consists of something like LOVE? However, in what it does tell us about the basis of existence, we indeed find **sure evidence** of the above. For instance, in the scientific world there is no certainty as to the **true nature of atoms** and sub-atomic particles, and the debate is swinging towards the idea that they merely are ***energy-charges***. Einstein said, "We have been all wrong. What we have called ***matter is energy***, whose vibration has been so lowered as to be perceptible to the senses, there is no matter." In addition, Max Planck, the founder of quantum theory, who, as a physicist has devoted his life to the research of atoms and sub-atomic particles, also said, "I am telling you that there is **no matter as such**. All matter arises and persists only due to a ***force*** causing atomic particles to vibrate, binding them in the tiniest of solar systems; the atom. Yet in the entire universe there is no force either intelligent or eternal; we must therefore assume that **behind** this force there **is an intelligent mind or spirit; the very origin of all matter**."

Just think: when extremely small particles without any real size or measurability are observed under an electron- microscope, one does not see a solid substance, but rather lively, ever-changing ***patterns of energy***. Furthermore, Quantum Physics has, over and over again, proven that we **cannot** strictly think of particles as **solid**, for they are **both solid and yet not solid**. As energy, they reveal features of both **solids** (objects, rocks and so on), and **waves**, such as are seen in water. It has been shown that sub-atomic particles can either behave as a solid substance, leaving marks when hitting a target, or waves, which have a much different effect (cf. the ***Two-slit Experiment***). They can be like **sand** that the wind blows against your feet, or **streams** of water that flow over them, or even ring-clouds which spatter light in all directions. They thus act as both particles and waves, and, while it is also not possible to measure both their position and momentum (where they are and what they do) at the same time, they simply seem to decide for themselves how to behave, and this cannot even be accurately predicted.

Electrons behave more like sound waves which move in all directions when striking a chord on a guitar. At times it was noticed that that the mere fact that they were **observed** during experiments changed their behavior; that when examined they acted like **particles**, but when left alone, more like **waves.** Experiments showed that it even appeared as if they are ***not there*** when unobserved, and the very act of observation in a way, actually creates them! From this some scientists have deduced that reality actually comes into being as a result of observation, and that what we see does not really exist; **no real world...** or, **different** worlds according to each person's perception! At present, however, it is said that it all depends on how the experiment is set up, the lighting used and so on, and the outcome has nothing to do with whether or not the process is observed. What is true, however, is that for different reasons everybody does not perceive the world in the same way (cf. Die Logos Liefdeskode). This does **not** mean that we can shape the nature of the world or our future by own perceptions or positive thinking, something many pseudo-scientific people advocate to enhance their own ideas.

Despite this, however, particles can behave so mysteriously that no-one truly understands them. This even had brilliant scientists like Einstein and Schrödinger raving! Schrödinger, referring to their experiments, remarked to Bohr: "Had I known that we were not going to get rid of this damned quantum jumping (particle to wave), I never would have involved myself in this business." And Bohr, who did excellent work in this field, said: **"Anyone who isn't shocked by quantum physics has not understood it."**

WHY SHOCKED? Because what we see as reality is not only energy that had ceased its wave-properties (the so-called ***"collapse of the wave-function"*** as to become particles), but uncertainty still envelopes the whole system, and it is not clear **how** they, in any way, can structure an **organized** whole. The sub-atomic world differs totally from, and is in no way similar to, what we see as structured reality. Although our bodily parts such as eyes and brains, and even objects such as houses, cars and so on, consist of them, particles do not have the fixed characteristics of the objects we see. It is as if they are totally uncontrolled and self-willed; yet they structure the **whole** of creation. What they are, and do, is so unpredictable that physics has actually formulated a basic law that states that all physical phenomena occur within a ***framework of uncertainty*** (the so-called ***"Heisenberg's Uncertainty Principle"***). No-one seems to be able to pin-point these sub-atomic particles, or knows what they are doing, and why.

Our world is thus in **no way** such a firm and fixed abode as we may think it is, and no-one can explain orderly existence without referring to **God**. Due to this, a frustrated Einstein said: "Quantum mechanics is very impressive, but an inner voice tells me that it is not yet the real thing. The theory produces a good deal, but hardly brings us closer to the ***secret of the Old One***. I am at all events convinced that ***God does not play dice with the universe.***" Einstein was thus convinced that there has to be a higher power and control in the universe! Richard Feynman summed it up by saying: "**No one** understands quantum mechanics. In fact, it is often said that of all theories proposed in this century, the **silliest** is quantum theory. Some say that the **only** thing that it has going for it, is that it is **unquestionably correct."**

Although we would have loved to say that science can truly explain what is at play in the universe, from these remarks we can surmise that science still only works with what seems to be truth, while the in-depth workings of the universe remain out of reach.

ENERGY-CHARGES?

In the light of this information, it is understandable that in the world of science there is an ongoing dispute, becoming louder and louder, on **whether atoms**, protons, neutrons and other sub-atomic particles, of which everything is said to consist, **really exist at all!**

The old atomic model was that atoms consist of a nucleon, surrounded by electrons circling it in trajectories similar to the planets orbiting the sun. Apart from electrons, science has since identified subatomic particles much smaller yet, so small that a thousand-million-million, all lined up, will fill the space taken by a single nucleon. These are called "quarks", with descriptions given to them such as ***up, down, charming, strange, bottom, top, truth, beauty, color and flavor***, as well as another group called "leptones", with names such as muon, tauon, meson, gluon and neutrinos. These all seem to haphazardly appear and vanish as they like.

The idea that these particles mimic the paths of the planets around the sun is no longer accepted. To science, at this stage, the structure of matter just is a theoretical model. Instead of following orbits, it is now assumed that these particles, which are never at one place at any time, present themselves as a type of haze surrounding the nucleus. Some scientists call them ***clouds***, others ***smears***, ***fields*** or even ***electronic fluids***, and now maintain that the idea of electrons remaining in fixed orbits is a figment of the imagination. Some even say they **do not exist at all**, but only show a ***potential to exist***. As Richard Feynman said, "No one understands quantum mechanics. The world of the miniscule doesn't obey laws we can describe;" implying that electrons are more a thought-concept than actual entities. Quantum physicist, Dr. Wolf, says that matter can no longer be seen as a substance, but only as a form of energy. The **deeper** we look into an atom, the **more it dissolves**, until we just see more and more particles swaying like wheat in the wind, connected with one another, and held in place by invisible waves; tiny shadowy balls dancing around in certain locations, sometimes changing position with their partners in perfect rhythm.

Even when focusing on the atom's nucleus, which at first seems a tiny dot, it too dissolves. It is also nothing more than a field or rhythmic wave. Inside the nucleus itself are **more** organized fields, smaller particles that, when examined, also dissolve into pure energy and movement. The **heart** of the world therefore has **no solidity**, ***only the dance of energy!*** There are ultimately no concrete objects, merely potentials and movement, shaped by electromagnetic fields coupled to other potentials. And this activity continues, while we know that all is ultimately just... ***energy!***

Actually, then, it is only energy that exists, while matter is not solid as it appears, but is just energy- or ***power-fields***. Perhaps we can best describe atoms as circular layers of energy similar to light auras or rainbows emanated from light towers, or simply state that matter is just fluctuating shades of activity. The recently discovered ***Higgs-Boson particle***, also named the *"God-particle"*, for which discovery Peter Higgs and Francois Englert were awarded with the Nobel Prize in physics in 2013, was also thought to make a contribution to explaining our existence. They theorized that there has to be a **fundamental particle** (or energy) that gives mass to others in the makeup of the stars and even our own bodies, and is able to bind and structure all matter. After all of the excitement and the money spent on the CERN collider, however, some scientists still maintain that the new discovery provides no real answers, and that we **still are in a crisis** regarding our understanding of the workings of the universe. Apparently even this particle can disintegrate in a shower or flash of light and is also referred to as the **Higgs**

field, an energy field that transmits mass to particles passing through it, thus giving them substance. This however, still does not answer any questions as to the origin of the universe. To whatever extent science benefits us, if we attempt to use only science to explain the origins of creation, we will always remain at our wits end.

Do particles exist, then? On the one hand, the answer has to be, "yes." How could they not be real if atoms make up our houses, hearts and the rest of natural creation? A subatomic particle beam (like a laser) can cut and tear things apart. It surely is real. Moreover, all mathematical and **chemical formulas**, as well as **equations** and **calculations**, only make sense (and are possible) because of the accepted existence and structure of atoms in certain quantities and proportions. These calculations have proven effective in industrial manufacturing, medicine and other production processes. Though some researchers believe atoms to be nonexistent, **something surely does exist**, but this appears to be more along the lines of ***fields of electrical charges in certain Quanta, or quantities***.

LOVE-CHARGES!

Everything becomes more beautiful if we, in line with the Bible, consider that everything was created **BY Love to BE love**. Atoms and particles are therefore, in reality, just ***love-charges***. Although everything has been hardened and subject to corruption since the curse, it is just energy given by God as to perform specific tasks; nothing else! What we see is a sublime essence passed on like light rays, which, in the end, becomes the energy that is converted into other forms. Atomic particles are then just energy, which represents the charges or fields which we call atoms. The **various forms** of energy/matter are therefore merely ***different patterns*** into which these fields have been organized. Everything then, is merely an interplay (now in a collapsed state), of ***vibrant love-energy*** in different nuances, (almost like different recipes), which, in power and wisdom, flow according to God's will and mind-concepts.

Each cell in a body, bird, flower or diamond is more like a song, with all the necessary notes and chords of love provided to spell it out, while the idea of particles or individual charges just completes the whole. ***Chemical formulas thus only portray diverse combinations of love-energy and how compositions of fluctuating quantities of this energy work together as to initiate "energeo", or perform, certain tasks!*** It also seems that everything consisted of nuances of this love-energy from the beginning, and only became the present structures we know that are corruptible and decay, since the fall. It also seems possible that, from the very beginning, everything merely consisted of ***nuances of pure love-energy***, and that only since the curse on sin, did decay enter and all became corrupted. It therefore appears that God originally designed energy-structures with which man would have been able to work creatively even had the fall not taken place, structures which have **now** become the different elements as we know them. As long as we keep in mind that, as has been mentioned above, it originally was not energy as we **now** know it, but an **unblemished, incorruptible** form.

This is not that difficult to understand, for in every task, such as composing or playing music, we have to apply the right combinations of power, rhythm and touch (e.g. on strings), in order to accurately mirror our feelings! The ability of energy to transform could also have existed before the fall, for this can occur according to God or man's will, and is not the same process as decay. Furthermore, had man not fallen, each person would still have used his/her own gifts so as to partake in work of a sublime nature, as we read that in heaven all shall serve God: "there shall be no more curse... and his servants shall serve him" (cf. Revelations 7:15, 22:3).

Although existence has been corrupted by sin, we still live in a ***power field*** emanated by God; the "works of his hands" (cf. Psalms 8:6). If everything is taken into account, energy just is emanated God-activity; "For **of** him, and **through** him, and **to** him, are **all** things: to whom be glory forever" (Romans 11:36).

Let's then consider this again: Life as described by the Bible and science is the works of the **same Creator**. What we see in the world and the universe are his ***mind-concepts*** becoming form and existence as He wishes it. We may then render ***strong*** in "love is strong" (Songs 8:6) with: Love is ***energetic energy***; powerful and able to do what it wants!

Diamonds, eyes, etc. (consisting of what **we** call atoms), and so spiritual attributes, just are different **shades of love** intermingling as to show what his wishes enfold! **Energy** then, is ***that kind of love*** science calls ***energy*** and ***that kind of love*** the Bible calls **mercy, meekness,** etc.; in the same way in which a smile or good heart is ***that kind of love*** **God calls *kindness***. Although ***love*** was corrupted by sin, it still shines through in multicolored facets in creation: in tulips, butterflies and even entire galaxies, all portraying God's qualities (cf. Romans 1:20). In the end, the energy our world consists of just is ***that kind of liveliness*** **we** call ***matter***, flowers or planets, that had become shades of **bad** energy. While "broken glory" resulted from the fall, what we now call atomic particles were originally flowing, cloud-like, soft and vibrant love-energies. **Pure love!**

Needless to say, this means that evolutionistic ideas about life resulting from atoms bonding together, should disappear completely from the scene!

4. THERMO-DYNAMICS: SCIENCE UNDERSCORES THE CURSE ON SIN!

Let me again stress that it is not science's duty to explain the reasons why unpleasant events occur or why everything is corruptible. Still, scientific evidence precisely underscores the message of the Bible. Had man not fallen into sin and were the curse not true, life as created by the God of love would still be **perfect**. Science, though, provides proof which is as clear as daylight, that this is true. This proof is seen in the **Laws of Thermodynamics** as accepted by scientists across the board. **No-one** doubts these laws which state that energy cannot be created or destroyed, and that it can only be redistributed or ***changed*** from one form to another.

As a scientific term, ***Thermo-dynamics*** is derived from "thermo", meaning "temperature" (think of a ***thermo***meter), and "dynamic", a word which represents working-power. What, though, does our existence and that of the cosmos have to do with temperature or heat? Everything, as without heat all the galaxies will freeze, life will die out and the entire universe will become an ice-landscape of dead stars and planets; just as without energy from the sun, the earth itself, and all of life on earth will likewise freeze.

How does one explain ***heat*** then? As already noted, all matter in the universe, whether in part or as a whole, is just ***energy at work.*** In physics, the same activity or energetic movement of particles is called heat and temperature. When we exercise we become hot and give off heat. It is the same with all of matter. Temperature is related to the rate of movement of electrons, and when heat is added, the movement becomes even more intense, temperatures rise and electrons are transferred to other atoms, repeating the process. We could equate this with children who, when they get excited, some jump about while others run away. When the temperature rises, electrons pulsate faster, releasing some to flow elsewhere. During heat- transfer, this happens in different ways: ***Conduction*** is a direct heat-transfer taking place between neighboring molecules, when the movement in particles at one end of a material object is passed on to others. ***Convection*** takes place when heat is spread by wind and sea streams flowing around the globe and also radiated through the cosmos, such as the electromagnetic radiation resulting from nuclear reactions in stars such as the sun. This can be in the form of heat, light, ultraviolet or other frequency waves. **Light and heat** just are different sections of the **same** electromagnetic spectrum.

Heat is transferred because, when there is an increase in temperature, the electrons or energy in a substance, or the system receiving it, oscillate faster. The thermal energy that is transferred is called heat. **Energy can thus also be described as heat, and heat, as energy.** From this research, we obtain thermo-dynamics, or the movement of heat! We can thus also call the laws of thermo-dynamics, the ***laws***

of heat-power. These laws describe the existence and movement of heat-energy in the cosmos. They explain the dynamics of heat, how it operates and spreads through vast masses of atoms by means of conduction, convection and radiation. In accordance with the ***Zeroth*** (basis) ***law***, heat will flow from objects or areas with a **higher**, to those with a **lower** temperature, until the two reach the same temperature and the heat-transfer will stop. At this stage they are said to be in thermal equilibrium. This is similar to two water tanks connected with a pipe at the bottom. The water will always flow from the fuller to the emptier tank until they are equally full. So also, heat moves from one system, (or part of a system), to another because of differences between the two. A practical example is when you put your hand around a mug of hot coffee. Your hand gets warm, but the coffee colder.

Electromagnetic radiation can also be carried along by light photons. ***Light*** is moving energy-charges that can cause ***heat***, just as heat tends to cause light. Energy can thus be likened to heat. And while energy is the ability to do work, to say that a body has a certain amount of heat-energy is the same as saying that it has a certain ability to perform work. In the human body a slice of bread can produce a certain amount of energy (heat) which provides your ability to work. **The cosmos as a whole is thus also like a vast factory producing and using heat-energy!** In order to get to the **crux** of the matter, let's examine two important explanations:

The **First Law** of Thermo-dynamics, also known as the law of conservation of energy, states that energy in a closed system cannot be created or destroyed. This means that the cosmos, as a ***closed system***, is like a full reservoir with a fixed amount of matter/energy that **cannot**

be added to, or augmented. ***Conservation*** in this case does not mean **saving** energy, but rather that the system maintains or conserves the **same quantity.** Matter can thus be converted into energy and vice-versa, but nothing is lost in the process; the total amount of energy in the universe remains the **same**.

Our **question** is: if man, as all evidence shows, does have a spirit, and energy cannot be created, where did the human spirit, consisting of (spiritual) energy, which includes aspects of intelligence, love and even hatred, actually originate? As will be seen later, love-energy can also be changed into hatred and vice versa. Logically, this spirit-energy could **not** have been shot out by exploding chemicals in a (physical) "Big Bang" event. Once we accept this, the shadow over the evolution theory darkens even further. Because energy cannot just appear out of nowhere or create itself, and if we accept that spiritual energy came first, the first law thus implies that there **IS a *source***, a creator.

This so-called "Big Bang theory" cannot even explain how a single mustard-seed can create itself! Even if the theory of an ***oscillating universe***, that all energy time and again (by loss of heat) becomes unusable and freeze, is then by gravitation drawn into a ***mustard seed*** as to again explode, were true, there initially must have been a Creator as to begin the process.

The ***Second Law*** of Thermodynamics underscores this. It states that all kinds of energy; whether potential, chemical, or kinetic, while constantly at flow and changing form, always becomes more dispersed and less organized. In other words, some of the energy that runs away like an overactive child to perform other work in the form of light or heat, is always lost. This is also called the ***Law of Entropy*** (the decay or breaking down of energy-matter), which continues by showing that this decay always gets worse until nothing (no heat) is left. This process is similar to the deterioration resulting from the "***collapse of glory***" which simply gets worse, as is universally evident. In our bodies, energy is converted into waste heat, sweat, excretion and so on, which all involves a loss. During the processes of rusting and decay, chemical compounds break down to form simpler compositions. No machine can be 100% efficient in converting fuel into power; some energy is always lost. In batteries (stored energy), the power eventually runs out. The working-ability of engine parts diminishes. The power and beauty of every flower, tree, animal or man eventually diminishes until they wither and die. The energy in stars like the sun will also eventually become exhausted. They are cooling down, and eventually this will result in increasing disorder in the universe.

It has been proven that energy cannot be destroyed. For example, when iron rusts, it reacts with oxygen to create iron oxide as a new compound, we call rust. As with all chemical reactions, though, **no energy is ever lost or gained**. Although now in different combinations, the **same atoms** from the original material are in the new compounds. The energy is still there, but over time, changes from usable to **unusable** and becomes unfit for further work, such as when materials are burnt and converted into smoke and ashes. The **quantity** of existing energy thus remains the same, but the **quality changes**. And the universe is running out of usable fuel; it is slowly dying a heat-death, while, as the Second Law of Thermo-dynamics informs us, the energy in the cosmos as a whole cannot be replenished! The Universe is thus running down like a battery that cannot be recharged!

It is then simply a scientific fact that an organised universe could not have developed out of chaos by itself, and be developing in an ***upward spiral*** as evolutionists allege. This second law directly contradicts any possibility of improvement, which makes **evolution impossible**. Moreover, as science argues, if the cosmos is 15 billion years old (as evolutionists believe), the entire universe, earth included, would, according to this law, have been depleted of usable energy long ago, and **all life wiped out**. This would surely have occurred during the time calculated since the so-called Big Bang up to the present time. So theoretically, all life should already have been wiped out! **According to science itself, evolution is thus not viable.**

Evolutionists, indeed, don't believe that the **whole** of the cosmos is improving. They maintain that, although the total amount of usable energy drops, the earth is **not** a ***closed system*** and gets enough energy from the sun so as to enable development and progression.

If the cosmos is as old as they claim, though, according to the second law of Thermo-dynamics, its many suns would have become colder and as a whole (earth included) it would surely have frozen long ago! In addition to this, the need for external sustenance sufficient to keep life going would have been so much greater! One can try to sidestep this, but the facts remain standing. The deepest truths that science teaches just underline the fact that God upholds all things by the power of His Word (cf. Hebrews 1:3).

THE HEART OF THE MATTER.

Our main argument, however, is the notion of **"entropy" itself.** God did **not** create something imperfect, enslaved to decay and corruption (cf. Genesis 1:31, Romans 8: 21). The laws of science as mentioned just underscore the truth of the Bible concerning man's fall into sin. No believer will indeed ascribe either the physical or moral corruption seen in the world to God. Even though those in the evolution debate tend to overlook man's fall, the teachings of the Bible on what the curse enfolds, is scientifically supported. We simply won't get a proper grip on life if we don't combine this evidence with what God has said concerning the reason for death, decay and corruption (cf. Genesis 3:17). Life is devouring itself from the inside out, and the book of Revelations provides us with His Word that the calamities will only worsen until He destroys all so as to bring about the new heavens and earth.

We can thus imagine the voice of God, who created the universe with just a spoken word (cf. Psalms 33:6), now uttering, after man's sin, a resounding call throughout all of creation; ***"cursed is earth!"*** This would have been followed by a shuddering wave sweeping through creation, distorting reality, twisting rules previously set in golden love, causing stars to explode, galaxies to lose form, and perfect love-energy to become chemical reactions which are prone to corruption and decay, imperfect mutations, bacteria, viruses, germs, defective DNA, even bad teeth and weak bones... a change that is impossible to fully describe, but a reality we know all too well!

Surprise! In the light of scientific knowledge, the words of the **Bible** are just **magnified**. In examining the findings of science, we see the same truths mirrored by the Bible, and in accepting what the Bible says on man's sin, we see how **true science** is. We are then freed from false ideas like a Big Bang or evolution. There is indeed no reason to doubt the word of God; all of life corresponds with it perfectly. When you look at something from all angles, consider all possibilities and arguments, and time and time again come to the same conclusion, you accept it as truth! This is how science and all courts of justice work. We may thus say that God's curse on sin can be taken as a scientifically- validated fact.

That this also holds true at the level of sub-atomic particles should come as no surprise. Where does the power and wisdom behind atomic structures originate anyway? Science does not busy itself with such questions, only with what can be seen and detected. However, not even science can explain why the ***"dance"*** of energy fields takes place, or even the source of energy itself. There are four major forces in physics: gravity, magnetism, electromagnetic forces and strong and weak nuclear forces, which all bind matter together. These are amazingly fine-tuned as atomic particle-clouds attached to each other. They hold the structure of substances together using the inter-mingling of different fields, so as to form elements that combine with others to form new substances.

No-one can say where these forces, or the power that causes particles to move, originate, without referring to God! In themselves these fields are **not** atoms; they just activate them. Had the subatomic world simply consisted of dead particles, matter would not have had the power to stay in closely-knit formations, to move according to fixed laws and to make heat, light and electricity possible. Now, however, although invisible, each force has its own existence and exerts a fearful power, able to combine perfectly with other forces so as to structure life and sustain beauty. All is just love, emanated by God!

This all means that the Bible is completely in line with science, but the theory of evolution does not fit with either of them!

SCIENTIFIC LANGUAGE IN THE BIBLE?

It is not true to say that the Bible does not use scientific language at all, when in fact, it does. For example, we read that "long ago God gave a command, and the heavens and earth were created **from water and by water**" (2 Peter 3:5). The text continues by saying that the elements will once burn and melt (verse 10). While the word "elements" in Greek refer to **fundamental parts**, and has been derived from a word meaning something orderly in arrangement, as in a series, just consider how orderly the **periodic scale** of elements is, and then note the depth of meaning behind these words.

It is a scientific fact that all substances consist of the **same** basic atomic structure, and the basis of all visible things is the **hydrogen** atom. All matter thus basically begins with Hydrogen. This term is derived from the Greek word for water; "***hudōr***"! The various elements only exist due to differences in the **number** of protons, neutrons and electrons which are present in their atomic structure, and change according to the activity of energy, that is, by **adding more** protons or electrons. Hydrogen, "H" in scientific language, is the simplest element, consisting of a nucleus with one proton and one neutron, around which one electron circles, while helium has two protons and two electrons. This continues throughout the table. Thus oxygen, "O" in symbolic language; the "O" in H2O, basically also consists of a mutation of the hydrogen atom, and later combines with hydrogen itself to form water (H2O). In other words, oxygen could be said to be derived from hydrogen as the simplest element.

The **basis** of our existence is thus **Hydrogen**, or water. It is also the closest that anyone without modern scientific knowledge could ever have come in describing the origin of elements. It is simply impossible that a fisherman from the first century, with no knowledge of science and atomic structure, could have used or even understood such specific and significant wording so as to indicate the creation as being ***from***, and ***by***, water (from the Greek "eks" and "dia"). As Peter writes, this text could only have been inspired by the Holy Spirit (1 Peter 1:21).

All the more interesting is that God refers to the ***love-energy*** as "water" even before the fall; ***living water*** flowing from under His throne (cf. Revelations 22:1). He is the source of energy, which flows like a stream from under His throne so as to make all of life flourish. Water (hydrogen) thus symbolizes the **energy** giving existence to the universe. Note that **all of creation began with water.** We easily overlook the fact that Genesis 1:2 reads that after creation, "the earth was without form, and void; and darkness was upon the face of the deep. And the Spirit of God moved upon the face of the **waters**" (cf. Genesis 1:2). Note also that almost the very first words regarding creation are that God **divided** the waters **below** from those **above** earth. First there was just a mass of water, then He said: "Let there be a firmament in the midst of the waters, and let it divide the waters from the waters." From the waters "above" the starry heavens were created (cf. Genesis 1:6,7), which directly shows that creation has **water as its basis**–not the "fallen" water we know since the curse, but the pure, flowing, love-energy of life.

The earth and heavens were thus made during the same stage. God began with water, divided it, and then from the waters beneath, created earth and from that above, all galactic bodies. Then a dramatic division followed, as water moved out into space to take form in galaxies and to follow the courses assigned to them! This not only **portrays earth as the center of the cosmos,** but shows how love-energy was deployed in a uniform manner to take on a million different forms (regarding the creation in six days, read “The Logos Code”).

5. FLASHES OF GLORY!

We may now attempt to better describe the beauty of the original creation. It is most important to understand that, with the ***"collapse of glory"*** entering only after man's sin, Adam could **neither** have been created from corruptible energy/matter, **or** have evolved as the result of chemical changes, mutations or other means, as these processes did not yet exist.

By merely speaking God first created the heavens and earth (cf. Psalms 33:6), displaying His love as a glassblower swiftly models a masterpiece in accordance with an idea (thought). The fact that Adam was created "From the **dust** of the earth" means that he was created from the **same** substance as the rest of creation, thus revealing his connectedness with earth (cf. Genesis 2:7). The words; "**From** the dust **of**," and not just, ***"from dust,"*** adds extra meaning, revealing a new aspect of energy that differed from the rest. Remember that this text cannot be referring to the earth or dust as we **now** know it, for the original creation differed from the present matter/energy. That "earth" must have been the then **still unblemished** love-energy! Let's therefore **not** say that man was created from ***dirt***, for God did not originally create dirt, so

Adam and Eve could not have been made from it. In the pristine state it was pure dazzling love shaping all of creation, while ***dirt***, a blemished beauty, only came into existence since the curse. Consider then how evolutionists maintain that everything developed from base chemicals that can rust and rot. This insults both God and human dignity! This argument completely eliminates evolution from the picture; simply because, with man first being created **perfect** and then falling into a material state, human development as evolution sees it is just a fantasy!

We can't compare Adam's body to that of Jesus as man, for He took on the form of fallen man in the accursed state, and was subjected to suffering and death, while Adam's body in the beginning was **not** like that at all. It was more like Jesus' body after his resurrection. Flashes of this glorious body can thus be seen when we consider Jesus' resurrected body. He is therefore, for good reason, called ***the last Adam***. The Greek word for ***last***, "eschatos" (Adam), therefore points to the intended Adam, or ***Adam as he was meant to be***. Paul is recorded as saying: "The first man Adam was made a living soul; the last Adam was made a quickening spirit; not first, which is spiritual, but that which is natural (as we now know man); and afterward that which is spiritual" (cf. 1 Corinthians 15:45, 46). This refers to Jesus' body after the resurrection that differed in quality from his previous form. After bearing the curse on sin and following his resurrection, He still had the appearance of a normal man and even ate with the disciples, but, being spiritual, could also pass through the walls of a room in which they were present and appear or disappear as He wished. Science tells us that the possibility of moving through a wall has to do with different tempos of vibration in matter; like high frequency radio waves when we talk on cell phones. This explanation given in the Bible, encompassed even more, as it showed that, after the resurrection, His body was totally different from ours. It was pure love-energy. The point made is that this text proves that the composition of energy/matter before the curse differed from what it is now, and **can again be restored** to the original glorious state.

Adam's composition at creation can thus be seen in Jesus' body after his resurrection, which represented Adam as he was originally ***meant to be***, but only after the effects of sin on pure love-energy were removed.

Moses' shining countenance after close communion with God was also so bright that the people could not look at him (literal translation; "his face was made in glory") cf. 2 Corinthians 3:7). This also shows that man's appearance can be **changed back** to radiant light if God so wishes (cf. "Scientific Backup" above). However, to what extent man as originally created in His image had a shining countenance such as that of Jesus at the transfiguration on the mount (cf. Matthew 17:2), we do not know. It still, however, must have been a body perfect in appearance and abilities. We can deduce something of these abilities from the fact that Adam, in power and wisdom, was able to **rule** over both the kingdoms of animal and plants, **name** all the species and remember them; something for which we now need computers! Bearing the image of God, He could, as ruler over all living things and tasked with subduing the earth, also could have had omniscience of what was going on right around the globe (cf. Genesis 1:28).

The fact that man's abilities were originally far more advanced and perfect also provides us with the **origin** of theology, philosophy, psychology, medicine and **all the sciences,** simply because our present lack of knowledge, insight and comprehension results from the corruption and limitations caused by sin. Had the fall not taken place, man, as created in the image of God, would have had unblemished wisdom in all spheres of existence. Although the beatific development of man's abilities and the unfolding of his wishes would surely have followed, it would have been regulated by divinely-inspired insight, producing perfect circumstances and results, **both** in what we call the fields of **theology and science**.

Before the fall man just had complete knowledge of God and life. From 1 Corinthians 1:30, "of him are ye in Christ Jesus, who is made unto us wisdom, righteousness and sanctification," we gather that man had lost his holiness, the ability to act righteously in God's eyes, as well as true knowledge, and can only regain it in Jesus. Now, however, neither theology nor science even comes close to knowing the full truth about life and existence, and in each field of knowledge, vast differences of opinion are experienced. As man has to now regain his previous knowledge of God, he has lost his understanding of what life and wisdom truly are. **All the sciences**, such as the social sciences, natural sciences, formal sciences such as mathematics, and applied sciences such as engineering and medicine, thus **result from man's fall** and the ***collapse of once- glorious knowledge.***

The same lack of insight applies to the understanding of our **spirit**. According to evolution, our existence is, as some call it, "a biological accident!" Did the spirit in man (cf. Job 32:8), complex as it is, also develop by accident? No! One can mix all the chemicals needed to make a human body, but will discover no life, thought or emotion in it.

So **where** does the spirit, which can experience all the nuances of love and hate, actually originate? Evolutionists, in stating that life began with the bonding of atoms, eventually leading to the formation of bodies, see the spirit as some obscure entity that arises from bodily processes. In demonstrating only a vague understanding of both its complexity and origin, they propose the idea that, as human beings learnt to understand the difference between right and wrong, intelligence, creativity and morality developed spontaneously. Our question though, should be; **from what** source of intelligence did it develop? As will later be seen in the section on DNA, the intelligence and knowledge involved could neither have been ejected by a Big Bang, nor have developed on its own.

As the Father of evolution, Darwin proposed that the spirit developed as the result of useful habits that paid off and were inherited by succeeding generations. He even suggested that some habits are perpetuated simply because they oppose others, or arise as the result of a build-up of tension in the nervous system, causing reactions such as joy or anger. Present evolutionary psychology argues that repeated encounters with certain situations were met with varying reactions. While some had positive results and others negative, man's mind was simply programmed to solve problems in pleasant ways, and these programs became the emotions designed to deal with the problems of life.

All of this would surely, if it occurred as evolution maintains, have led to ongoing moral development and improvement. As this is certainly **not** the case, and we do not have a morally- perfected man or a morally-enhanced society, we will have to think further!

BODY AND SPIRIT: A UNITY!

As we read in the text; "man became a living **soul**" (cf. Genesis 2:7), man was created as a unity of body and spirit from the start. Once we understand this, we will also see that the Bible is correct and thus able to refute evolutionistic ideas that human life began with chemicals, which then developed into a body, and finally, something like a spirit. The simple fact is that the spirit has **nothing** to do with atoms, which can neither combine with, nor improve on it. Even the "spiritual lives" of chimpanzees, which are purported to be the most ***highly-developed*** living beings next to man, are a very far cry from our own. The Biblical text informing us that body and spirit came into being as a **unity**, however, just further underlines the fact that man has **not** developed through a process of evolution.

The description of ***soul*** in the Bible does not point to something separate in us, but is a term for the **complete** man as a **unity** of body and spirit. (Soul is described by the word "nephesh" in the Hebrew Old Testament texts and "psuche" in the Greek translation of the New Testament). This term is used about 800 times, and in by far the most cases, simply refers to the person as a whole; my/your/his/her soul, which is the same as; me/you/he/she as a person. God does not say that we **have *souls***, but **are** living souls, and there is no duality of body and spirit as we tend to see it, rather a unity (originally) consisting of the same perfect energy. The soul is therefore just a compilation of different nuances of love-energy.

Adam, on being formed from dust, comprised the complete make-up of man as a living soul, as proven by the fact that **both** his body and spirit were energized by eating fruit from trees. Paul echoes this by saying that Adam was made a living soul, ***"of the earth, earthy!"*** (cf. 1 Corinthians 15:45, 47). His complete soul as a body-spirit union was of the earth, or rather, the original unblemished dust of the earth, revealing a closely-knit union, to which sin (as will be discussed later), has brought about a separation;. for afterwards only the body lived from earthly food. Body and spirit were thus created as one and will remain one.

Also note that the ***breath of life*** blown into Adam **was not** and **did not create** his soul; it just brought **life** to it. The accent in the text; "The LORD... breathed into his nostrils the breath of life; and man became a living soul" (Genesis 2:7), falls on "living". Having been created as soul, the breath of life just endowed life so as to make him a living soul. This statement is confirmed during the creation of Eve, who as complete soul, was created in a moment (the Hebrew word means "built") from a rib from Adam's side; showing that even a part of Adam was both body and spirit, and that becoming a soul and being given life went hand in hand. Emphasizing this, Genesis 1:20-24 records that animals, birds and fish are also made from dust and also became **living souls** (The Hebrew word is "nefesh"). Although it is not mentioned in the text that the breath of life ("neshamah") was blown into them, as is the case with Eve, Genesis 7:21-22 (in the Hebrew texts), shows that it was also in **all** life "that moved upon the earth: fowl, beast and of every creeping thing that creepeth upon the earth." We even read that, as energy taking on new forms, the waters "brought forth fish and every living creature after his kind" so effortlessly that it seems as if water actually ***gave birth*** to these life forms (Genesis 1:21). In line with what was said regarding the water, note that, "the **waters** brought forth" all living creatures; also birds. At the almighty command, there was merely an **energy change**, they came into existence and simply appeared. The fact that they, like Eve, became living beings the moment they were brought forth, supports the standpoint that all creatures were immediately formed as **body/spirit unities** (cf. Ecclesiastes 3:19 and "The Logos Code").

Very important is that the entire universe was created by the Spirit of God (His "ruach"; cf. Psalms 33:6), and man's spirit is also called "ruach" (cf. Genesis 41:8). The breath blown into him which brought life, though, was not called "ruach", but "***neshamah***" (cf. Genesis 2:7); a word we find in 23 different verses (cf. 7: 22, Job 27:3, Is 2:22 and Daniel 10:17). Beholding God, Daniel lost all strength and there was no "neshamah" left in him; no vitality; as if dead! His **spirit** was still in him, but he was rendered feeble and powerless (cf. Revelations 1:17). The breath of life given by the Spirit of God is thus **different** from man's spirit and another nuance of energy, empowering souls with life. This means that life in man is **not the Spirit of God** Himself. When man sinned, God Himself was **not** defiled, and when man spiritually died, it was **not** the Spirit of God that died! "Neshamah" was thus a new nuance of love-energy on the scene, able to give life! (We will return later to what this tells us about DNA).

PSYCHOSOMATIC EVIDENCE!

Supporting the standpoint that body and spirit is a unity, whilst scorning evolutionistic ideas, are the so-called Psychosomatic (spirit-body) illnesses. This concept is derived from "psuché" (soul), and "soma" (body). When either the body or spirit suffers, it is directly experienced in the **entire** soul. Research shows that every emotion sends out waves (energy-fields), affecting the physical brain, heart, liver and other organs, also opening or restricting arteries, leading to other feelings such as sadness, loneliness and fear, or even physical states such as stress and fatigue. Suppressed anger can damage the nervous, cardiovascular and immune systems, cause indigestion, allergies, ulcers and a long list of other diseases. Studies show that up to 80% of illnesses are spirit-body related; brought on by emotions such as anger, hostility and grief. This all suggests a unity of body, mind and spirit, underlined by the fact that that pain-killers, anti-depressants and alcohol (**chemicals**), are able to influence and deaden **both** body and spirit. Also note that all bodily as well as spiritual anomalies involve changes in chemical (atomic) compositions, such as facial changes when blushing or experiencing anxiety. Even so-called mental diseases are treated with chemicals consisting of atomic compounds.

Because all anguish stems from sin, medication is thus not our primary need. As Carl Menninger (psychiatrist) said: if only people in mental institutions could believe that their sins were forgiven, 90% of them would walk out healthy that same day. (For a more complete exposition of this aspect, read "Die Logos Liefdeskode"). All these facts reflect the evolutionists' vague understanding of the complexity of man, as well as the impossibility of its tenets.

SIN: LOVE-ENERGY TURNED BAD!

Needless to say, evolution not only denies the existence of sin, but can in no way explain man's corruptness. Where do crime and violence, and destructive emotions such as jealousy and hatred spring from? And why is it that these do not exist to the same degree in different people, who have **all** developed along the same path?

What then, is sin? From an understanding of the unity of the spirit-body it is now easy to conclude that the same corruptness involves both body and spirit, as can clearly be seen in human behaviour. This also applies to all of the love-energy from which everything was created, including emotion. Being created **by** Love to **be** love, everything actually consists of emotion. As indicated above, the word emotion is derived from the Latin word "emovere", where e- (ex-) means "out," and "movere", "to move," thus the ***in and out***-flowing movement is one and the same. Thoughts, emotions and beliefs also consist of sublime energy, as we read in, "the motions of sin work (energeō) in our members"; "God works (energēma) a diversity of gifts of the Spirit in all" (cf. 1 Corinthians 12:6-11), and "He works (energeō) in us both to will and to do (energeō) of his good pleasure" (cf. Philippians 2:13); that is, to love and to act with love as He wishes. Negative emotions are therefore **love-energy which has been corrupted.**

Some people believe that emotions, as mere feelings, cannot be right or wrong, good or bad. How, though, can hatred, jealousy, covetousness and other destructive emotions not be wrong and sin? Even being **angry** is seen as **murder** in God's eyes (cf. Matthew 5:21, 22). In the case of emotions such as anxiety, jealousy, overzealousness and pride and actions such as dishonesty, and violence, we can clearly see how they obstruct love and are therefore sinful.

"Sin" as described in the Bible, primarily means to ***"miss the mark"***; such as when archers miss a target. We can comprehend this more fully when we examine what happened at man's fall. Everything taken from its life-sustaining source will wither or die; such as fish removed from the water or plants from the soil. In sinning man shifted from being **pure love** and moved into the **sphere of evil** and death. As mentioned above, sour milk still consists of the same atoms (energy) as fresh milk, but is no longer usable. In the same way, man has become ungodly (cf. Romans 5:6). And the picture gets even worse if we think of rotten meat. However repulsive it may be to compare man to this, rotting also results from man's fall, and the fact that these states in man and meat are equally disgusting, can be seen in the many acts of murder, rape, and abuse we are exposed to daily, as well as the promise of sin's eternal punishment, "Where their worm dieth not" (Mark 9:46). **Sin is** therefore a corruption of pure love-energy; **love turned bad!** The energy has not stopped working; it has just become depraved, and can now only be described as hatred, and this life as death; unusable by God!

As I said, true life as created by God died the day man sinned (cf. Ephesians 2:1,5-6), and natural man could now be described as a living embodiment of "love gone bad!" Sin then, is not something external that leaves man intact. **Man himself** has become the arrow that misses the target. And hatred is not the opposite of love. Love, in its original form no longer exists after the fall. Man can still **love**, but this ***love*** is polluted by hate. Just as a ruined painting is not the opposite of what it was; it is the **same** painting, **just defaced**. What then about the love we see in those who have not yet been saved? Hatred may present itself as love, but before this corrupted energy-state is restored by the person being reborn, it can never be pure love. What natural man calls "love" in all its many shades, is just selfishness. Such a person knows what appears virtuous, is pleasing to others, and is rewarded, and then acts purely for those reasons; to look noble, to be praised and to enjoy the adulations of others. This means that "***good***" people, when still not saved, are still ***missing the target***. By living for themselves and not God, their lives are merely concerned with their own glory; which is still living in sin. Sin is therefore NOT just wrong deeds, but ***which we are not***, that is, no longer the image of the God of love. Sin is not just ***mistakes*** that are made and later "corrected" so that he can proceed unscathed, but involves the **entire soul**, which has now become **a wayward arrow**, missing the mark. Sin is to have stopped being love! In this statement we also see how the theory of evolution misses the mark!

CAN ROCKS SMILE?

Was Jesus just joking or being nonsensical when He said, "I say unto you, that God is able of these stones to raise up children unto Abraham?" (Luke 3:8). Surely not! He was speaking as the Son of God and almighty Creator. Did He not, in the beginning, also basically use ***dust*** to create man? From the fallen energy in stones, He could indeed have raised fallen men such as those he was addressing. And how wonderful it is, when observing man, to still see "dust" coming alive; simply because **atoms are not dead** but **active energy**.

As mentioned before, when experiments and observation provide overwhelming evidence, science accepts it as truth until it is proven wrong. We can then better understand how atoms, like man's spirit, are still ***energetic love-charges***, but since man's fall, have been corrupted. Were they dead, they would not be able to embrace life or transfer it during procreation. Now, though, **atoms** are not only energy being sustained by the breath of life, but are also able to **feel** and **express emotion**; which once again, reveals the unity between body and spirit.

The atoms in our bodies are of the same make-up as those in rocks, but in the case of our bodies, have been shaped into retinae, ear-drums, nerve-tissue and other sense-organs, allowing us to experience this jam-packed phantasy of life, hearing, seeing, smelling, talking and relishing all varieties of emotion. Atoms thus account for our senses of sight, sound, thoughts and feeling. Moreover, the joy awakened by pleasant experiences such as music is also the result of the atoms in receptor-cells, but in this case, these feelings activate the **spirit**. All this can clearly ***not*** arise from something that is dead. To love or feel loved differs totally from that which we call atoms, yet the smell of a beloved's skin or touch of the lips brings on a multitude of feelings. What we, as a result of atomic structures, see, hear and feel, directly affects our emotional state.

Emotions such as love and hatred as other nuances of energy, can express themselves through such structures, producing a smile or a grin. When the breath of life enters it, dust becomes a living part of the soul; as it **not mere dust**, but ultimately, ***vitality from God.*** Dust can therefore take form and have the ability to listen, work, and think, either lovingly or resentfully!

Consider the fact that thoughts and feelings in themselves are not atoms, but can cause headaches, tension and ulcers in the body, affect one's health or even produce a feeling of bliss... in ***atoms***. The slightest wave of emotion experienced by the spirit is exactly mirrored by atoms in up to a 100 small muscles in the face; while the eyes, the ***windows of the soul***, portray all of our feelings. All the more interesting is that a red face when angry, a smiling face when happy, or a blushing face when ashamed, also involves intricate **chemical changes** in the body, chemical reactions which form neuro-chemicals. This occurs whether we experience love, hate, or some other powerful emotion. If all of life was just chemical reactions between atoms, we would be able to take pills containing chemicals so as to experience love, joy and bliss, which we **cannot!**

Bodily organs fit seamlessly with the spirit, which is why **chemicals** as energy-charges are used as medicine for maladies such as **depression**! And where do the feelings of hunger and thirst originate? Mere dust, as in a stone, cannot get hungry. Why would dead atoms, simply fulfilling a function, cry out for energy so much that the bodily cravings can drive us (the spirit) crazy? Note that they don't pass energy on in the same way as before with the transfer of heat or like an electric current, but we experience a **need**; a need which can also apply to the hunger for love, peace or justice. Actually there is not a relationship between body and spirit; they are simply a harmonious unity. We **are spirit** embodied in (what we describe as) chemicals.

Furthermore, notice how perfectly ***love-charges*** fit in with science's explanation of ***energy-charges***. Although we cannot pinpoint it, this is where the sub-atomic quark particles called "**up**", "**down**", "**strange**", "**colour**", "**beauty**" and so on, must come into play; mirroring all emotions by means of facial muscles and feelings.

What gives gloss to life are precisely traits such as softness, friendliness, charity, flavor and beauty, all positive and metaphorically "UP", while "DOWN" would (metaphorically) relate to depression and other negative states of mind. This just shows the depths of energy-flow that can be contained in ***atoms!*** All of this once again reveals that body and spirit is a unity, merely consisting of different shades of energy.

How great is the realization that a defiled spirit can be cleansed (cf. Psalms 51:10). All of energy, including negative emotions and the corruption of man's spirit, can still be ***changed back to glory.*** Paul says, "But we all, with open face beholding as in a glass the glory of the Lord, are changed into the same image from glory to glory, even as by the Spirit of the Lord" (2 Corinthians 3:18). Note that just as energy can be converted into other forms, the original love-energy was converted into hatred, but by the spirit of God, can also be converted from hatred **back** to love! This is why true conversion is a change of heart. In terms of pure science it makes sense, doesn't it?

When Jesus says "Bring forth therefore fruits worthy of repentance, and begin not to say within yourselves, we have Abraham to our father: for I say unto you, that God is able of these stones to raise up children unto Abraham" (Luke 3:8), He uses the Greek word "metanoia" (repentance), which means **reformation** or **reversal**. As in the miracle of the loaves and fishes, He can indeed, in a moment, convert stone into all the chemicals required for life, as well as blow the breath of (new) life into it! People with hearts like stone (cf. Mark 6:52), may again bear the fruit of the spirit and become loving and kind.

MORE ON EMOTION!

As I said, the statement "God is love" means that emotion, as that which "moves" in one, including thoughts and feelings, is also **energy** and a **physical**, vibrant and powerful substance. This is also true of

God. The Bible refers to God's soul 14 times and ascribes to him about 50 emotions. As mentioned in ***The Logos Code***, Jesus is the ***express image of God*** (cf. Hebrews 1:3). The Greek word for "express image" (charaktér), can be explained as follows: if you press a stamp with a rose on it down on paper, it will portray an exact copy of the rose. He is, "the Image of the Invisible God", and as Creator merely expressed Himself in what He Himself created. As Love, He poured out his soul in creation. Jesus thus not only displays God's character, but shiningly portrays His attributes in all of creation surrounding us. Although it is now mostly drowned in the harshness of energy's fallen state and difficult to detect, we are in reality, surrounded by the God of love, exerting love-energy. In creating, He imprinted the ***character stamp*** of His personality onto the cosmos (cf. John 1:3, 14:9, Hebrews 1:3), as if He Himself is the stamp which showers us with all of love's beautiful traits.

We thus experience Him in the twitter of birds, the fragrance of flowers, loving hearts and other aspects of creation. While all of creation was simply created as shades of love, the wholesome goodness of God as love can be seen in a smile, tasted in honey, smelt in flowers, heard in music, expressed by our tongues; all carried by a shroud of atoms that we, in the light of what has been said, may call a flashing flamboyancy born from love. To envision the core-essence of life we should not consider galaxies, gold, health... or pain, but rather God's warm heart, beauty and happiness. The crux of our existence is a saccharine phantasy of tender kindness; a golden love-dream emanated by Him!

God is love also means that He displays His attributes in creation! When He smiles, heavens declare it, and when He is angry, we are troubled (cf. Psalms 104:29); which does not show Him in a bad light, as His emotions are motivated by a mindset of pure love, and we should not project our concept of imperfect love onto Him. He hates sin and punishes it, but His emotions are just and never misplaced.

All of this shows that the present atomic structure of things was neither part of man's original state, nor were there originally only atoms, with the spirit developing later. The basis of all existence, stronger than any solid state we now know, was originally meant to be softer than wool and sweeter than honey, a sweet dream and supple manifestation of kindness; the placid music of love. Had man not fallen, the original glory of nuances of love-energy would have been experienced in every minute detail of life, as the elegant glow of sheer affection, **as it is in heaven**; translucently effusing into that which God wished. **Imagine then**, the sparkling fairyland of this pristine state, where shades of energy, glowing, frolicking, singing and translucently shining from the inside out, as to materialize in His mind as concepts of man and nature; life as it ***was meant to be!*** How glorious flowers, birds and nature were then, and will be again after the renewal of the heavens and earth! And this renewal applies to you as well!

MORE ON THE BODY-SPIRIT UNITY!

The fact that man, from the beginning, was created as a union consisting of sublime nuances of love-energy and **not flesh and blood**, further **defeats evolutionistic claims** that man was flesh and blood that developed biologically, and that the spirit developed later. When Paul says "flesh and blood cannot inherit the kingdom of God; neither doth corruption inherit incorruption" (1 Corinthians 15:50), he refers to the corruptible flesh and blood body which results from man's fallen state. Life in heaven, when restored to what it ***was meant to b***e, is total bliss, and man won't need this corruptible body any longer. Like angels and those persons in heaven, man, before his fall, surely did not live from oxygen, but by the spirit of God which upholds life, and blood was therefore not needed to convey this oxygen through the body. **Blood**, like **all internal organs** consisting of chemicals, thus stems from the curse. This was necessary because, in a cursed creation, as **collapsed** love-energy, everything now had to work in such a way that man could think, eat, hear and so on, as well as take in oxygen and excrete waste energy. Note the important role **eating** plays in the curse on sin: "Cursed is earth" and then: "In the sweat of thy face shalt thou **eat** bread" (Genesis 3:19). Eating and energizing is the core of life. Except for oxygen, all of man's intestines, stomach, liver, spleen, gall bladder and kidneys, only have to do with **food** and its digestion!

This also applies to man's **brain**. It is important that the Bible does not even mention the brain, only the ***mind***; further revealing the oneness of body and spirit. Paul speaks of "the ***spirit of the mind***," saying, "be renewed in the spirit of your mind" (that is, learn to **think** in a new way; Ephesians 4:23), and, "The spirit in man **knows** what is in him" (cf. 1 Corinthians 2:11). Without the spirit, the brain, consisting of atoms, is dead. After the death of the body, the chemicals constituting it are still the same, but the body is now lifeless, while the spirit of the deceased still knows all he knew before. The rich man, after death, could indeed remember his brothers and how he lived while on earth (cf. Luke 16:25, 28, Revelations 1:7), again showing that in the beginning, the soul was a living unity, but of a much higher state than after man had fallen.

From Paul's words we can deduce that the mind is just a part of the spirit, or the workings of the spiritual energy which constitutes the spirit. As Dr. L. Dossey says, "The mind steadfastly refuses to behave locally, as scientific evidence shows, brain-like tissue is found throughout the body." We may ask: when a thorn penetrates the flesh, what gives **cells** the wisdom to form those substances that surround it so as to expel it? This wisdom needed for the brain to give such instructions, and the cells to receive and carry out these instructions, will be even greater when it is the spirit of the mind itself acting in these situations.

The author personally knew somebody who had lost all feeling and nerve function in one arm after suffering a stroke. He taught himself, though, to give his arm and hand commands to reach out and grab, and the hand would only let go again when he told it to do so, something no medical practitioner could explain. Because man's spirit is actually in charge of the body, we can readily accept that this happened, because his spirit **overrode** the normal neurological path of commands from the **brain**, proving the existence of a ***super-structure*** surpassing fallen man's bodily functions.

In the light of all that has been said so far, our conclusion is that all of man's organs, whether those dealing with thinking, eating, or other processes, are themselves the result of the change brought about by the fall, and thus prone to degeneration and disease. The curse on sin touches **all** of love-energy as it was created. This again shows that atoms are merely ***love-charges*** that have been corrupted and as one ages, it becomes worse. In the end, all of life's unpleasantness and ailments are spirit-body disease resulting from the ***fall from glory***; love-energy that has been corrupted. This is why, without an understanding of the fact that germs and viruses are volatile units of corrupted energy, their source will remain undetected. Everything that we are now, and will later become even more deficient, results from the curse. The theory of **evolution** will **never** be able to explain it. Disease is simply part of sin's make-up.

The Bible treats sin and disease as one, and compares healing with forgiveness by God. In truth, **sin IS the disease** and disease itself proves body and spirit to be a unity, as it was created. This is also why we can be healed by Jesus' wounds. The fact that He was; "Wounded for our transgressions, and with his stripes we are healed" (Isaiah 53:5), indicates that He suffered on the cross so as to take away all bodily and spiritual disease. Healing, even of unbelievers, **only** results from this action; as in the case of the nine lepers who did not return to thank Him (cf. Luke 17:17). Had God not, after man's fall, prearranged the cross, He could immediately have thrown man into damnation. All of history unfolds only because of the cross, and if even unbelievers are healed, either directly or by taking medicine, it is simply because also the price has been paid for them as well, and God in His love and tolerance, gives them a chance to return to Him. This does not mean that we can, in every case, attribute disease to specific sins, for by means of suffering also those who are forgiven, are chastised and kept humble. (cf. Deuteronomy 8:2-6). The aim, however, is to bring people to the cross and to the only Healer.

WHAT BEFALLS ENERGY AT DEATH?

Needless to say, not only can evolution in no way explain how **death** fits into the system, it directly contradicts the idea of ongoing improvement. We may ask why it is that particles which (according to this theory), in some very intelligent way have decided to group logically so as to form eyes and the complex organs of living beings, have not also developed the ability to keep the body permanently healthy!? Why is God's **curse** on sin the **only** explanation that man can give for pain, agony and death?!

Having shown that only the Bible provides real answers, we may also ask what happens to the body and spirit at death. In observing the process of death, it appears as if the body remains behind while the spirit leaves. According to the prevailing belief, this means that people who have died cannot have already attained new bodies.

Our question is whether the Bible actually teaches that body and spirit are separated at death and will only be ***reconciled*** again at Jesus' second coming. In this case, what really happens to energy at death?

As far as we're concerned there is no real separation. From what the Bible says, we can make some deductions; which again, all refute evolution. **First**, it is important to repeat that God does not say that man, in the beginning, was body and spirit, or that there was any disparity between them. The spirit could not have developed later, for man just was created as a ***living soul*** (Genesis 2:7). Paul's account of the difference between the bodies of Adam and Jesus, using the terms "natural" (soma psychikon; psyche; soul, with a soma- body), and "spiritual" (soma pneumatikon), underlines the fact that body and spirit was, is, and after departing from earthly life still will be, a union, needing no reuniting. Paul says: "There is a natural body, and there is a spiritual body. It is sown a natural body; it is raised a spiritual body." The first man Adam was made a living soul; the last Adam was made a quickening spirit" (1Corinthians 15:44-46). When Paul says that at death a natural body is "sown" in the ground (verse 44), it cannot mean he was created as a "natural" body that could die, for death only followed **after** the fall. That which God created as man, is, in the next verse (45), described as a "living soul" (psuchen zosan)(Genesis 2:7). Man was thus initially not able to die, but following the fall, now can, while his spiritual body is raised in power (verse 43). Man's fall thus caused the living soul to become a "soma psychikon" or natural body that could die. "Natural body" thus refers to the body of man as sinner, that can die, and, "spiritual body" (soma pneumatikon) to the body believers obtain **after** death. This is emphasized in Joshua 3:15 and Judges 19, where "psuchikos" is used to describe the "fleshly" life-style of sinners. Adam was created a "living soul" (psychen dzosan), but **not** a **sinner**. He became a "soma psychikon" by sinning. When Paul says then that his body was, "of the earth, earthy; the last Adam is the Lord from heaven" (1 Corinthians 15:47), he refers to Adam's creation as perfect man (psuchen zosan); from the still unblemished energy, the original ***dust of the earth***.

"Earthy" does therefore not refer to an earthly, mortal body, as opposed to a heavenly body, but indicates that it was like the rest of creation **before** it was changed by the curse. In the beginning Adam thus had a body like that of Jesus **after** his resurrection, and both Adam's initial body and Jesus' resurrection body consisted of flawless love-energy. As the ***Second Adam***, after His resurrection Jesus thus embodied a living soul (psychen dzosan). Because He is also God and not mere man, Paul writes that He became a "***quickening*** (zoopoioun: life-giving) Spirit"; a spiritual Being able to **impart** new life to spiritually dead people (verse

45). The word "Spirit" then, points to His exalted nature as a giver of life (cf. 1 Corinthians 15:21: "As the Father raiseth up the dead, and quickeneth them, even so the Son quickeneth whom he will".

This means that had man not fallen into sin resulting in death, there would have been ***no inequity*** between body and spirit, and man, as such, would have lived gloriously forever. Each of Adam's descendants would then also have been a "living soul" (psychen dzosan). The difference in how body and spirit now are nourished causes them to appear as separate, when in fact they are a unity. Prior to sin **both** were vitalized by fruit from trees. As we read in the text; "cursed is the ground for thy sake" (Genesis 3:17), the "collapse of glory" encompassed all of creation. Since the curse, fruit and man's body now consist of the **same atomic structure**, which proves that **all** of creation underwent a change. While man's spirit has become equally corrupted, and now requires nutrition in the form of faith, the fact that the body now requires fruit and vegetables, causes them to **appear** as if they are separate entities, which they are not. The curse thus also resulted in a differentiation in what happens to different shades of energy at death.

Further note that we normally see life in the body as physical, as opposed to the life hereafter as spiritual existence. The distinction between "natural" and spiritual (cf. 1 Corinthians 15:44), though, is **not the same** as that between **physical** and **spiritual**. In other words, it does not mean that man is raised **without** a physical body. As already stated, both are strong and physical, but not "physical" opposed to "spiritual" as we tend to understand it. While the word "natural" (psychikon) refers to sinful man, Paul contrasts sinful, earthly life with the life hereafter, as fully governed by the Spirit, but refers to a ***body*** (soma) in both cases, saying that life hereafter is also in a body.

Should we then (wrongly) view "psychikon" (natural) as the present physical body as opposed to the coming spiritual body, it will prevent us from understanding that people in heaven are already complete, having **real**, physical bodies; not needing to be reconciled to other bodies! The reason why Paul refers to deceased believers as; "the ***spirits*** of just men made perfect" (Hebrews 12:23), may precisely be because they do have bodies (sōma pneumatikon), in the same way as **angels** also **have bodies**, but are called "***spirits***" (cf. 1:14).

The fact that Moses and Elijah visited Jesus in visible bodies from heaven on the mountain (cf. Matthew 17:2, 3), tells us that they already had heavenly bodies. Also, the fact that Paul writes that a spiritual **body** (cf. 1 Corinthians 15:44) is "raised" after being "sown" (buried), means that, after death, a believer is still in a ***body***. In the parable of the rich man and Lazarus, after death the rich man says that he is, "tormented in this flame," and asks if Lazarus could be sent to dip his finger in water and cool his tongue. This implies that, although his earthly body had been buried, he **still has** a (suffering) body, and that body and spirit remains a unity (cf. Luke 16: 24,25).

It does therefore not seem as if a body will only be given back to the spirit at the final resurrection. The soul remains in a spirit-body union. With Paul already stating that that which is raised is a "body", what can be **added** to this body by reconciling it with the old? Nothing! It surely **won't** become a body of ***flesh and blood*** again, for that exactly is what stays behind: "Flesh and blood **cannot** inherit the kingdom of God; neither doth corruption inherit incorruption" (1 Corinthians 15:50). Man will not need reconciliation with his old body in the same way as the ***new earth*** will not need the old. What will happen is that the changes wrought by the curse on sin will simply be corrected.

Believers who at death, are immediately taken to heaven, will thus also have bodies, for a **body** is raised up; with the difference that it can no longer feel pain, or be imperfect in love. This will be a spiritual body, raised in glory and power (cf. 1 Corinthians 15: 42, 43), perfectly able to see, touch, eat, hear, and so on, but eternally flawless. A life of full vitality, free from all limitations and living in a blissful reality, as it was before man's fall. Paul says "we shall be changed" (1 Corinthians 15:51, 52) and our bodies will be "transfigured" to that of the "image of God's son" (cf. Philippiians 3:21, Romans 6:5, 8:29). "We shall be like Him; for we shall see him as He is"; shall be equal to his resurrected body, while those who are still living at His coming, will be changed in the twinkling of an eye (cf. 1 Corinthians 15:52).

When Jesus says; "the hour is coming, in the which all that are in the graves shall hear His voice, and shall come forth; they that have done good, unto the resurrection of life; and they that have done evil, unto the resurrection of damnation" (John 5:28-29), it does **not** mean that only ***bodies*** will rise from the grave so as to be reunited with their spirits, but rather that all people will rise to their final destination. If we accept that we are immediately taken up in glory at death, as He told the man on the cross, "**Today** shalt thou be with me in paradise," and in the light of verse 24, "He that heareth my word, and believeth on him that sent me, hath everlasting life, shall not come into condemnation, but is passed from death unto life," then John 5:28-29 merely means that on hearing His word and accepting or rejecting Him, each person is instantly judged; and enters either into the resurrection of life or damnation. The verse that states; "The... dead shall hear his voice and they that hear shall live," can indeed only refer to **spiritually** dead persons, as believers already share in everlasting or heavenly life (cf. Ephesians 2:5,6, Jo 3:18).

This is underscored by the fact that, after being reborn while still on earth, the **body** is **already** renewed. In the text; "Christ is formed in us... He quickens our mortal bodies by his Spirit that dwelleth in us" (Galatians 4:19, Romans 8:12), Paul talks about God's resurrecting power working in our earthly lives, dissolving the desires of the flesh and bringing the body into line to serve Him with all of its abilities (cf. 12:1). Having been crucified with Jesus, the old body of the reborn man is already dead: "Knowing... that the old man is crucified with Him, that the body of sin (the body of the old self which, under its own power only served sin) might be destroyed, that henceforth we should not serve sin" (6:6). Now that Christ is in us the body is dead because of sin; but the Spirit is life because of righteousness" (8:10). As Paul says: "though our outward man perishes, yet the inward man is renewed day by day" (cf. 2 Corinthians 4:16). "Without Jesus in us, the body is dead as to do good, but we now are alive for God" (cf. John 15: 4,5). These texts reveal that **both** the sinful body and spirit, being already crucified with Jesus, are renewed.

In the end these texts also help us to see how **logical** the **resurrection** is. Without sin there would not have been corruption, whether in life or in the grave. Jesus' body immediately changed from flesh and blood to a glorified one, with nothing remaining in the grave to support the idea of a **later** reconciliation of body and spirit. This logically means that Jesus' resurrected body neither required blood nor oxygen for Him to live. When Paul says He became a, "life-giving spirit" (1 Corinthians 15:45), he talks about a resurrected state in a body that could still clearly be seen, but calls Him a **spirit**. He Himself said, though, that He was **not** a bodiless spirit; "Behold my hands and feet, that it is I myself; handle me, and see; for a spirit hath not flesh and bones, as ye see me have" (Luke 24:39). We also read that David was buried "and saw corruption" (Acts 13:36). He saw (experienced) that the outer garment of the body at death is reduced to dust. Regarding Jesus, though, he prophesied, "thou wilt **not** suffer thine Holy One to **see corruption**" (Psalms 16:10, cf. Acts 2:31), because He Himself was not a sinner. He took on a body of flesh and blood, was subjected to suffering, but His soul, as body *and* spirit, were not corrupted. The punishment for our sin was passed on to Him, but He had no sin, and was always just pure love (cf. Hebrews 4:15).

The point is, because Jesus' soul, body and spirit, was without sin, after He had atoned for, and removed sin, He was resurrected **without anything being left behind in the grave**. As God He could not die, but as a man, he eradicated sin by dying to atone for it: "God sending his own Son in the likeness of sinful flesh, and for sin, condemned sin in the flesh" (Romans 8:3). This is also why He could have been "transfigured" on the mountain; his face shining as the sun" (cf. Matthew 17:2). All of these details again prove that sin brought"harshness" to both body and spirit, as can be seen in the fact that Adam and Eve tried to cover their disgraced bodies. In this we can clearly detect their ruined spirits in the shame, fear and broken companionship they experienced.

This means that neither man's spirit nor body will cease to exist, but be changed as a unity. In the case of believers, changed to glory by a final cleansing, or else sent to damnation. What stays behind at death is only the ***harsh covering*** of corrupted elements resulting from the fall, which makes it **seem** as if it is a separate body that remains. In fact, this "body" is just corrupted energy returning to dust, which, under the "bondage of corruption", is taken up in other forms (Romans 8:21), and which will be taken away at Jesus' coming; when, "the heavens shall pass away with a great noise and the elements shall melt with fervent heat" (2 Peter 3:10). Then all will be changed back to pure love-energy, bringing about new heavens and a new earth. The corruption of energy will thus permanently fall away.

This does not mean that man has a ***body within a body***, or another body as a ***sub-stratum*** in and behind the visible body. The body we see after death is just is the **atomic structure** that was nurtured by food from nature that will eventually disintegrate, as is the case with **all** of the cosmos. Without making final statements, it seems that at death the real man inside the biological structure is simply ***extracted*** from the harsh, corrupted outer garment (which clothes the entire cosmos); extracted like **cream from milk.** What remains are only crude elements, the "leftovers" that will finally be eliminated at Jesus' coming; like a crust on a wound that falls away once it heals.

At death only the outer crusts remain, while the sinful body-spirit continues to exist; with those of believers being changed to glory, and those of unbelievers proceeding to eternal doom. Up to that point, however, man first has to "***see corruption***" and witness the results of his sin to the very end, as seen in all forms of ageing, destruction and worldly rot assailing the outer man.

PRISTINE AND COMING GLORY!

What will happen to natural beauty such as roses and butterflies in the afterlife? Using the scientific evidence uncovered, we may now also say that, according to the Bible, **everything will return to love-energy** as originally **unstained** by sin. How beautiful life will be in glorified bodies, when all tears, sorrow and death have passed away! Glorious it was in the beginning, and glorious it will again become! Man's body will be the same, and yet not quite the same; a glorified, incorruptible body (cf. 1 Corinthians 15:35-43). As explained by the laws of Thermodynamics, we are now subject to corruption: disease, ageing and death; while heavenly life is immune to such destructive powers; incorruptible and beautiful like eternally fresh flowers (cf. 1 Peter 1:4; from the Greek word "amarantos", unfading!) In other words, "glorious": blissful, vigorous, perfectly healthy and with a radiant gloss and beauty as restored to God's image: "it bears the image of the heavenly" (cf. 1 Corinthians 15:49). It has "power", vitality, and is a "spiritual" body, not existing of atoms, but recreated according to what man ***was meant to be*** (cf. verse 44). We will be like Jesus (cf. 1 John 3:2).

Note that **nothing** God has created will just **disappear** or cease to exist. All living beings have an eternal existence and will, either in the heavenly sphere, or that of damnation, continue to exist eternally; which applies to both body and spirit! After death believers' bodies are timelessly renewed, while those of unbelievers enter eternal corruption (cf. Daniel 12:2). Unbelievers, as body-spirits, are already dead to God, and after death, after seeing the destruction of the chemical components of the body, the unbeliever will simply enter eternal corruption. Although corruption also holds true for the "outer" structure of the bodies of believers, they, renewed in both, move on into a state of perfection. Such a man once again becomes a "***living soul***" (psuchen zosan). All energy will thus be changed either into a better or corrupted (worse) form! As I said, the old heavens and earth will not be replaced, they will merely be ***renewed***. The Greek word "kainos," as in, "I make all things new" (Revelations 21:5), does not mean the same as, "neos" (new), as if it had not existed before, but rather, gloriously refreshed and "new in character." It will just be, "changed" (Hebrews 1:12). In a similar manner, the bodies of believers also will be changed to those of glory (cf. 1 Corinthians 15: 50-53). A re-creation; not a new one!

Unbelievers will be tormented forever (Revelations 20:10), and continue "in shame and everlasting contempt" (Daniel 12:2). These will be hateful souls in revolting, spiritual bodies; in a state of eternal decomposition, fully experiencing their own hatred as punishment. For the children of God, though, death and resurrection is a final cleansing of corrupted energy so as to return it to beauty. What decays in the earth or rises as gasses at cremation, is corrupted energy, awaiting the day when all of creation will be renewed and the energy of decayed bodies consisted of will be taken away so as to purify it of harsh corruptness.

Imagine seeing yourself in a mirror, no longer flesh and blood but having a spiritual, angel-like body, ablaze with jubilant love, all your characteristics are now pure and amiable and nothing blurs this perfection. The only experiences that you won't find in heaven are tears, death, stress or pain (cf. Revelations 21:4). No blind, deaf or lame people, no crutches, quadriplegics, hospitals or cemeteries: "Behold, I create new heavens and a new earth: and the former shall not be remembered nor come into mind... I create Jerusalem a rejoicing, and her people a joy. And the voice of weeping shall be no more heard in her" (cf. Isaiah 35:10, 65:17-19).

This "All new" surely **includes plant-, bird- and animal life** (cf. Revelations 21:5). "The earnest expectation of the creature waiteth for the manifestation of the sons of God. The whole creation groaneth and travaileth in pain together until now. But also shall be delivered from the bondage of corruption into the glorious liberty of the children of God" (cf. Romans 8:19,22). Paul adds, "The creature was made subject to vanity, but, the **creature itself** also shall be delivered from the bondage of corruption into glorious liberty, **just like** the children of God" (verses 20,21). All life still suffers under pain and death, but "God has given a **promise** of hope... creation will be freed from corruption," to enjoy the same freedom as the children of God. It is a promise; the most sublime is yet to come; a return to radiant glory! A creation free from death, mourning, hunger, thirst and heat (cf. Revelations 7:14-17). Plants and animals also suffer under the curse on sin; all experience agony and death. They also sigh and endure the pangs of birth, and are bound to this life, slaves of a harsh process which includes dying. God's promise of a better life therefore includes them.

Behold the lilies, the doves, and other creatures; **the most beautiful is yet to come**, when all of life will be as free from anguish as the children of God, jubilant and flawless before his throne... "Wolf and lamb shall feed together, and the lion eat straw like the bullock" (Isaiah 11:6–9, 65: 25). Another flash of the coming pristine glory! A time will come without the present bloodshed in the animal kingdom that also entered through man's sin. Children will play with animals now considered dangerous, while cows and bears will eat the same food as do lion and oxen; heralding a return to the original glory in which Eden is restored (cf. Genesis 1:29,30). **How glorious** butterflies, flowers and birds must have been, and will be again after the renewal of the heavens and earth!

INFINITE HEIGHTS!

There is yet more to keep in mind. To be able to deduce what we will be like from a description of Jesus' body after His resurrection is not that simple. Without changing His essential being, He was clearly able to take on any form he needed to fulfill his purpose of declaring God to man (cf. John 1;14). He could appear or vanish at will, move through closed doors and also eat normally (cf. Luke 24:43). Both before and after the resurrection, at different times, people were able to recognize Him, and at other times, not. Some saw Him as a gardener, a ghost or a stranger (cf. Mark 6:49, John 20:15, Luke 24: 31). At His ascension He was taken up into heaven in the body they knew (cf. Acts 1:11; 3:21), but in Revelations 1 we see of Him appearing in His full glory, "His head and hairs white as wool, as snow; his eyes as a flame of fire," and we hear that his glory is so immense that a sun is not needed in heaven, for **He** himself **is the lamp** which enlightens all (cf. 21:23).

As the Son of God whose love shone through the humble lampshade of his humanity, He thus both before and after the resurrection, used various methods of revealing Himself. In 1 Corinthians 15: 41-54, we read that believers' bodies in heaven will be even more glorious than that of Jesus' when appearing to His followers after the resurrection. "We shall be like him; for we shall see him as he (now) is" (1 John 3:2). John therefore points to a state of being far higher than his appearance on earth; a glorious being of light and power (cf. 1 John 1:5). As He said, we will be **like angels** (cf. Matthew 22:30).

All of what has been said on man's origin and the unity of body and soul directly **refutes evolution**. While the Biblical rendering is true, all of evolution's teachings are false. Also consider the grave danger that the theory enfolds; blinding people from the truth that everyone will have to face God in eternal light.

6. THE GENETIC CODE!

However much the Genetic code may amaze us, **only** the **Bible** can explain its origin! What a statement! ***Genetic*** is yet another key scientific term taken from the Greek New Testament, where the word "***genos***" is used to denote race or kin. This shows our true origin and how scientific knowledge of genetics supports the Bible. Evolution, on the other hand, again misses the mark! This book, as mentioned, is primarily intended for believers, as it seems to be impossible to try to convince evolutionists that something as complex as DNA could **not** have evolved by itself, and that apart from seeking the answers in God, the source of such vast stores of genetic information has never been found. They laugh it off, offer some weak explanations of how step-by-step changes in simple life-forms resulted in what we see today, and otherwise merely hope that further evidence will be discovered one day to prove them right.

In encountering the genetic code, however, we need to face some straightforward facts:

First, **no-one** on earth can truly fathom the depths of DNA, and studying it just emphasizes how extremely complex it is. DNA is the genetic information encoded in body-cells that programs each new living being so as to determine race, build, personality, health, how organisms will be assembled and function and so on. You could call it the ***program*** or in-built prescription that governs the growth and development of living beings and their bodily components, including their activities and procreation, a recipe that is passed on from parent to child.

Second, although what the **Bible** teaches is also above human understanding and a matter of faith, it provides a **complete**, and by far the best explanation of the **origin** of life that one can hope to find. As will be seen, the Bible not only provides answers for the origin of DNA, but we can learn much more from it than from any other research done in the field! Before we get to the answer, it must be said that DNA presents evolution with its greatest dilemma and points to their losing the battle! However much they try, the theory of evolution cannot explain the origin of the genetic code, without which the existence of living beings is impossible. According to evolution, life has a spontaneous origin that started with the grouping together of atoms to form the first molecules and cells, which then divided and reproduced, to eventually form nucleotides, consisting of atomic compounds linked together to form a DNA molecule that can replicate itself. They claim that this then formed amino acid chains with certain functions, and all of this took place over millions of years.

However, not only is it **impossible** that such complexity, ending in such a positive outcome, could have happened by ***chance***, but the possibility of molecules replicating themselves requires intelligent processes which are beyond their explanation. When a cell divides, a copy of the DNA is first formed inside the cell. Then small needles develop that take the new DNA to its opposite side, whereupon the cell splits to create an exact copy of itself, and the process is repeated ad- infinitum. The main question, though, is **where** the information that it carries, actually came from? A speck of DNA contains enough coded information to fill a million books. It surely does not come from natural processes, for it commands and directs those processes. DNA can be compared to a ***management plan*** which is there to arrange all the body parts and organs in living beings. How can such precise and complex information develop by chance, creep into matter/energy and then shape it? Energy itself has **no intellect** or ability to **create** information, and it surely could not have been shot out by the Big Bang? DNA actually informs the **atoms** what to **be** and what to **do**. Without it, nothing takes place in life. To bring this all together requires a level of intelligence beyond our present imagination.

As mentioned in ***The Logos Code***, atoms acts like a **truck** carrying a load of **DNA-manuals** in which the truck's **own** colour, shape, parts and operation are described. The manuals themselves, though, can in no way bring it into existence, control its parts and repair breakdowns! Yet, **this** is how atoms and DNA function in our bodies! Atoms and DNA information differ totally from each other and are structured according to different logic, scientific facts and spiritual knowledge. The chemicals in DNA are comprised of sugar, phosphates and bases, but the atomic matter does **not** contain the actual **information**, it only carries the information which controls the process which governs the composition and growth of bodies, it's functioning, and the correction of ailments. DNA thus controls the atoms, but is itself **not** composed of atoms or bound to their laws.

Evolution claims that microscopic beings came into existence by molecules spontaneously grouping together and then these groupings somehow managed to ***find* the code** for the later construction of bodies, process of digestion, ears, eyes and so on, and delicately **build it into its own DNA**, ensuring its own future existence. For every change in development, the DNA itself would also have needed improvement, which is **impossible**, as the DNA itself **manages** this development! Babies born **according to** the genetic code, encoded to continue the process, is the only viable explanation!

Information programmed into a computer cannot be compared to this, for it does not cause the computer to exist, procreate or fix itself. The program information is only is an electronic process by which it is instructed to give **back** what was fed into it; it does not depict the type, shape and characteristics of the computer; which is what the genetic code does. Dr Werner Gitt, an expert in the field, calls the genetic code the **best proof of creation by God**: "The cells of the human body can produce at least 100,000 different types of proteins, each with a unique function. The information to make each of these machines is stored on the molecule, DNA. It has never been shown that a coding system and information could originate by itself through matter... information studies predict that this will **never** be possible. A purely material origin of life is thus ruled out"!

Moreover, the ***truck*** and ***manuals*** cannot exist without each other and must have been formed (created) **together**. DNA: Nucleonic Acid (the NA in DNA or Deoxyribonucleic acid), stores information as to also instruct the development of life-important protein (nourishment consisting of carbon, hydrogen, oxygen and other products), in the same way as one would manufacture fuel for the truck); while protein itself (the truck carrying the manuals), is needed for forming of Nucleonic Acid. **Both** thus had to be present **from the beginnings of life**. Even if life did start with atoms grouping together, this cannot explain why **250 different kinds** of cells (brain-, bone- and others), are shaped, controlled and correctly placed by something ***totally different*** from itself. ***Something*** must then have been able to see to it that ***"by chance"*** the needed DNA-information is present to form **all** kinds of cells needed as to fulfill all of a body's needs, and that all of them are correctly situated as to **fulfill a dream!**

According to evolution the development from one life-form to others happened because of the competition to survive called "***natural selection***," and and changes by "mutations."

To say that everything arises from a struggle to survive means that the most basic life forms must have instructed their **own** DNA to change as to improve and be better than others; which is impossible, for they they themselves were constituted by their DNA. DNA-information cannot simply develop by itself or progress from nothing to higher levels of functioning, as it **contains** only that information with which to develop its living host. In other words, a **mutation cannot add** information to the genetic code.

Because DNA-information cannot by itself develop from nothing to higher levels, for it exactly contains the information to **make** living things grow, a **mutation cannot *add*** information to the genetic code. No new information can come from natural selection. Furthermore, the argument that living things evolved as the result of mutations which slowly changed the features of living creatures so as to become new forms, is equally impossible! A mutation happens when the DNA is being copied and is similar to a **copy-mistake** in a **recipe** (view the genetic code as an instruction-manual for life). The result is that during the division of cells and procreation, the **wrong** information is transferred. Such a process cannot add information, and mutations would therefore actually **destroy** existing information. Mutations always lead to a loss in information that may cause deformity and illnesses which can be carried over to descendants. While evolutionists say that mutations result in changes into higher life-forms, scientific research proves that mutations cannot bring about **any** such improvements. No mutation has ever been found that has added to the volume of genetic information or has improved on the ***recipe***.

According to evolution there must have been a stage at which living beings were originally chemicals that wondrously came to life, and subsequently had **no** brain cells, liver or other organs. The complex information-code needed in forming these, in the light of the above research, thus had to be present from the beginning and could **not** have been added later. The question is therefore, where did this code originate? **Was** the information there from the beginning, however, it would have caused complex life forms from start on; **which exactly is what happened!** As mentioned in ***The Logos Code***, Trilobites, which are supposed to be one of the **first** life-forms ever, were **extremely complex** beings with hearts, multifaceted eyes, circulation-, digestion- and intricate nerve systems and antennae. All life-forms were indeed very complex from the very beginning! Moreover, the same quality of information exists in **bacteria** and plants as in persons. Unicellular bacteria and algae that, according to evolutionists, were some of the **very**

first life-forms, surely have shorter genetic codes. But the fact of the matter is that they have genetic instructions **just as complex** as that of human beings. Again, this could not have happened over millions of years, as this **same code** still determines the composition of these bacteria and algae.

Evolutionists are aware of these insurmountable problems, but cannot solve them. To top it all, they can in **no** way explain where and how life originated. "Natural selection" only describes the process of improvement on previous life forms, but not where **life itself** began. The mystery is that when a heart stops, the genetic code and atomic structure of the body are still the **same** as before, but **life has gone!** It is given and taken away by something higher than nature. All of this is vested in the ***true genos code!***

THE ANSWER!

So where does DNA actually originate? Is there a **genetic link** between **man** and **God** as Creator? **Yes**. All men were meant to be children of God, but Jesus, as ***only begotten*** (from the Greek word monogenẽs: from "mono" (only), and "**genos**" (offspring; and described by J.O. Buswell as "**the only of his kind**"), son of the Father is the **uniquely** born, only true, direct, son and "express image of God," displaying his **complete** personality (cf. John 1:14,18). As mentioned previously, the Greek word for "express image" ("character", cf. Hebrews 1:3), can be interpreted as: if you press a stamp with a rose on it on paper, it will portray an exact copy of the rose. So He is, "the image of the invisible God, **firstborn** of every creature" (Colossians 1:15). Being firstborn of every creature does **not** mean that He was created, for **He** created all things (verse 16), but, similar to the ***firstborn*** in Old Testament times, He is ***first in rank***; and as the first of a series, depicts the rest, He was the ***blueprint*** in whose image man was created. The word "Firstborn" (from the Greek: "prototokos"-prototype), attests to this, showing that He is paramount above creation, whilst the words "**Only begotten**", combined with, "**Firstborn of every creature**," indicate that He is both the only real Son of God and the model of all of mankind that proceeded from HIm, the unique forerunner of all others! Had man not fallen into sin, his attributes would clearly have been seen in us as well, as created in the ***image of God***.

We note that in Ezekiel's striking vision of the ***Man in God***, the only body parts that are named, are his **loins**, portraying power and especially **procreative power** (cf. Ezekiel 1:26: "Upon the likeness of the throne was the likeness as the appearance of a man above upon it." Further, Genesis 35: 11; 1 Kings 8:19; Acts 2: 30; Hebrews 7:5, 7:10; Strong's Dictionary). He is thus depicted as the ***Giver of lives.*** We also read: "the souls that came with Jacob, which came out of his **loins**" (Genesis 46:26), and, "kings shall come out of thy **loins**" (Genesis 35:11; Genesis 46:26; 1 Kings 8:19; Acts 2:30; Hebrews 7:5,10). Because we spring from His loins, Paul says, "in him we live, move, and have our being. For **we are also his offspring**" (from the Greek "genos": Acts 17:28).

This is beautiful: **we are God's offspring!** We may think that it's just a way of speaking, but it's not; this is what God has said. Note Paul's argument: "**because** we are his offspring we should not think that He is like gold, silver or stone ..." (verse 29). We know this because **He can be seen in us**, originally made in his image! Psalms 8:5 portrays man as a little lower than a godly being, crowned with glory. Although subordinate, we don't realize how godlike man was supposed to be. Before originally being born, we were ***in his loins*** and when Adam sinned, all of mankind was still **in his loins**; now to be born as sinners (cf. Psalms 51:5, Romans 5:12). When Jesus was resurrected, He was once again; "the firstborn among many brethren". All reborn people were ***in his loins***, so as to be brought back to life and "conformed to his image, that he might be the firstborn from the dead, and firstborn among many brethren" (cf. Colossians 1:18, Romans 8:29). The fact that Ezekiel saw Jesus as the ***man in God*** not only reveals why He could become man like us, but that He had created man according to his image. What an immense difference from believing that mankind stems from ***chimps and apes!***

The link between God and man is thus most beautiful. He created man as soul (man as a body-spirit unity. Cf. Genesis 2:7) from the same energy as the rest of the cosmos, and breathed the ***breath of life*** into him, bringing him to life. As mentioned above, this breath **was not**, and did **not create** his soul, but just brought him life so as to make him "a **living** soul." Note again that although the entire universe was created by the Spirit of God ("ruach" cf. Psalms 33:6), the "breath" that brought beings to life, is not called "ruach" but "**neshamah**" (cf. Genesis 2:7; 7: 22, Job 27:3, Isaiah 2:22). The breath of life is thus something given by the Spirit of God other than His spirit: a different nuance of energy, empowering souls with life. Further, and just as important, is the fact that that the "breath of live*s*" (neshamah), blown into Adam, in Hebrew is in the **plural** (cf. Genesis 2:7), means that, thanks to procreation, from the first created life and breath of life blown into Adam, more "live*s*" could come into being. This, coupled with the unity of body and spirit, can also be seen in the creation of Eve, who was created as a complete person (from the Hebrew word for "built") from a **rib** from Adam's side. This shows that becoming a soul and receiving life goes hand in hand. As created from Adam, the "neshama" or life-principle was **already** in her. And so were Cain and Abel born as complete living souls and body/spirit unities. The differences we now observe only result from the "collapse of glory".

UNIQUE PERSONALITIES!

The phrases "God formed man," and, "breath of lives," thus encompass a wealth of meaning and say much more than to merely refer to a body with its organs. "Neshamah" as the breath which bestows life, must simultaneously have brought in **individuality**, which brings us back to what was said previously, that the forming of, and giving of life to man, was one act. All of creation was formed by God, yet we can clearly see that in stars, butterflies and other forms of nature, the word "formed" includes the multifaceted, **individual properties** of each life-form, with all the details ***formatted*** so as to produce the completed "**beauty in diversity**" that we see in the full display of creation.

To what extent each parent, as in the case of Adam and Eve's children, contributes to the forming of each new personality by means of DNA carried on by sperm- and egg-cells, no-one can tell. Eve, as a unique soul, was created from Adam's rib, which already carried the DNA. In fact, all human beings have the same genes, but no two people have the same versions ("alleles") of it. Evolutionists take the ***sameness*** of genes as proof of development within the same groupings, but cannot explain the **varying** capacities amongst people. If evolution were true, **why** are all progeny not exactly the same? Clearly, each person is curiously "wrought" in a mother (cf. Psalms 139:15), while it is God who measures out each's attributes according to His plan. We may then conclude that that which ***we call DNA*** existed in a sublime form from the beginning and that it can be directly linked to the "***neshamah***, "breath of lives", the activity which gives life and carries God's encoding. This can be confirmed by the fact that the **rib** from which Eve was formed contained all the elements needed for the formation of a human being. If what we call atoms, as previously mentioned, are just ***Love-charges***, it now makes the most perfect sense. What **we** call ***DNA*** is just part of the make-up of the harshness that entered the world through sin, causing us to think of it as something other than God's own code for the creation of man. Initially it was just ***spiritual energy***, or "Neshamah": God's genetic code of love energy, meant to, although no two persons are exactly alike, pass on his image.

If it had not been blemished, we would, though unique, just have portrayed God's personality! He clearly endows people with different "shades" of love-energy as attributes or gifts of the Spirit, a love seasoned by God, each "shade" having specific capacities built into the particular DNA encoding. To be an image of someone, however, means to be **just like him**, and to reveal him by means of your own characteristics. It can be none other! Man was thus created to be a living portrayal of God–even of his eternal nature, in the sense that we will never cease to exist. Mirroring God's attributes such as omnipotence and omnipresence, the original (perfect) Adam's abilities must have empowered him to command everything on the earthly plane, to know what was going on around the globe. For example, we read that he could name and remember the names of all animals and had the power and wisdom to reign over the earth and all living things (cf. Genesis 1:28).

Although man can never become God, like the small hand of a child in his father's, Adam received His personality, including His attributes. To envisage what He is like is thus only possible because we can view Him in the characteristics which He wakens again in believers who are witnesses to his unblemished love. Had He totally differed from us, we would neither have been able to identify **Him** or **with** Him. In Jesus, "the image of the invisible God, the firstborn of every creature" (Colossians 1:15), we see our source and how we should have been. We thus understand ourselves by understanding our Creator. We should have been "express images" of His person; resembling Him in righteousness, faithfulness, love and mercy (cf. 1 Timothy 6:11)! As the result of either awe or ignorance, we tend to see a **vast gap** between God and us, causing us to feel isolated from Him, while, although we owe Him humble submission, it is only our sinfulness that causes the sense of such a ***gap***.

Whether God creates a new spirit at each person's conception, only the body is inherited, or a spirit-body received from the parents, is an old dilemma. Clearly an identical body is not inherited, for, in defiance of evolution, **each** body is always **new**, while evidently, certain bodily traits can be inherited. This **also** applies to the **spirit**. As seen in negative emotions and spiritual suffering, the harshness that came with sin clearly does not only affect the body, but even more so, the spirit.

If we, in debating whether the spirit is also inherited, **distinguish** between body and spirit, we end up in confusion. Viewing the spirit-body as a **unity** makes it easier to see that, just as the body has certain traits and may suffer from certain hereditary diseases, the spirit may also carry certain propensities, character traits, musical or mathematical abilities, weaknesses and so on, that are genetically carried forward. This may not be the same in all cases, or to the same extent. Each unique spirit may, at conception, also receive characteristics that his ancestors perhaps did **not** have. What is passed on therefore, does not just relate to the body, but to the **broken image of Go**d, man as a soul. This proves that the spirit, as corrupted energy, is also carried forward to later generations.

Had God created a new spirit every time, it would have been pure and sinless, for He cannot create sinners, and it could then not have been said that man is "conceived" and "born" in sin (cf. Psalms 51:5), or, "as by one man sin entered into the world, and death by sin; so death **passed upon all men**, for that all have sinned" (Romans 5:12). It is therefore not true that, as sin is not a material substance, but a moral corruption, it cannot be inherited. It is the **same *energy*** carried by its predecessors. Remember that the information carried by DNA, as the code for the formation of souls (body and spirit), is not substance like atoms. It actually **IS spirit**. It is thus all a matter of **corrupted energy** (livelyness) **being procreated.**

As I said, "breath of lives" means that during procreation, more distinct lives come into being, which means that mankind has **one basic soul**, which, after being corrupted, carried the corruption forward as indicated in Romans 5:12. As the creator of each new soul, God uses what He has previously created, but endows each with a **unique** encoding by adding or withholding certain qualities. Note therefore, that **Adam** as the first soul, was endowed with all the attributes of mind, power and wisdom with which to fulfill his purpose as representative of God, yet he also had a separate personality. **Eve**, by just being a woman, already had **unique** qualities. Their children were also unique, differing in abilities and potential. One became an agriculturist and the other farmed with animals. As Eve was created from Adam, and Cain and Abel were, in turn, also individuals and differed in body and spirit, each person which followed is therefore also ***similar yet unique***. This is the miracle of creation. During human procreation God still creates, and in His wisdom can form each rose from the same stem unique in shape and fragrance. Although each individual essentially receives the same soul, he or she is given different shades of Love-energy.

The fact that the Father, "giveth not the Spirit ***by measure***" unto Jesus (cf. John 3:34; Colossians 2:9), means that as a man, He had the **full set** of talents that could **possibly** be given to man, not a measured portion as other persons receive. As his offspring (cf. Acts 17:28), though, each soul is given a ***measure*** of specific characteristics and abilities so as to fulfill a role and bring about a functional society (cf. Ephesians 4:7; Romans 12:3). The True "***Genos***" supplies the coding, equipping all persons with a specific purpose in mind. Each won't have the same power, wisdom and abilities, but each is given a ***grouping*** of gifts in different measures. The DNA of each person is therefore uniquely encoded, for example, as seen in that Bezaleel and Aholiab, by the spirit of God, were endowed with wisdom and knowledge to do skilled works in gold, silver and other precious metals (cf. Exodus 31:2-5, 1 Corinthians 7:7, 1 Peter 4:10), while Solomon was especially gifted with wisdom and Samson with strength and power.

In the parable, Jesus informed us that one person was given **five** talents, another **two**, and another **one**; to every man "according to his several ability" (cf. Matthew 25:15). In this context, it would be acceptable to exchange the word "abilities" with "**meaning**". In other words, each receives a unique set of gifts with which to deploy God's special meaning for his/her life (cf. Daniel 1:4). Unbelievers also have special abilities and attributes, but differ from believers in that they use these for ***selfish*** ends, which is why Jesus explained how the servant with the wrong attitude buried his talent in the earth (cf. Matthew 25:18). It was given by God to serve Him, but he just used it for own purposes. He only had one, for his life as ***singularity*** in total was lost to God.

As can often be seen, once they come to faith, God uses the gifts such as musical talents or accounting skills each soul already had in his service. He may, however, bestow on them additional gifts such as intercession, teaching and prayer. The old talents are also **renewed** while fresh skills are **added**. In the end, the smooth functioning of society and congregations depends on members using their different gifts to this end (cf. Ephesians 4:7, 1 Corinthians 12).

This again portrays the perfect logic of Jesus' becoming man so as to save us. He did **not** have to undergo a **change** in order to do so, because He always was the ***blueprint*** in whose image man was created. In the light of what has been said on love-energy and the vast difference between God and man only entering with man's fall, no fundamental change was needed for Jesus to become man. Nothing was added to his person, for He portrayed the **full** splendor of God, having all the God-attributes as imparted to man, but also already perfect man; as Ezekiel saw Him, the ***Man in God!***

However, we may well ask how He appeared when He took a rib from Adam and brought Eve to him (cf. Genesis 2:22), and in what form was He when He talked to them about the trees, slaughtered animals and dressed them? The Hebrew text reads that He ***wrapped*** it ***around them*** (cf. Genesis 3:21), which is like the actions of a normal man, as was the case when He wrestled with Jacob (cf. Genesis 32:30).

7. TIME AND ETERNITY!

It is a simple fact that the main factor needed for the gradual development of life forms as maintained by evolution, is **time**. While evolutionists believe that the first living species developed about **four billion years ago**, the vital question is whether the earth really is that old. In the end we will show that this can**not** be true.

We first of all need an explanation of how time as we know it can be reconciled with an eternal God; and the Bible indeed provides enough information so as to guide us. Though it is not at all simple, that the **Eternal** God became man in Jesus, going through **earthly** time, means that time and eternity **has** to be **ONE** and coupled with Him. As the Eternal He indeed became one with and acted in our time; showing that this is what happens all along!

How can this be explained? As said in "***Die Logos Liefdeskode***", Einstein's theories on time cannot help us. If we could, according to the idea of **time warps**, either shrink or stretch earthly time to a millionth or million times what we currently experience, this time will **still differ** from God's eternality. Even if time dilation could occur and people in different parts of the cosmos would have experienced time differently, in the end makes no difference to the outcome, for unity exists on another level (some more remarks on time in the rest of the cosmos follow later).

♥ I AM!

In this regard Jesus made a vital remark: "Before Abraham **was**, I **Am**" (John 8:58). He did **not** say, "Before Abraham **was**, I **was**," which from a historic viewpoint is also true, for as God, He indeed existed before Abraham lived on earth. He says though, "I (**now**) Am before Abraham", which actually means, "I am God eternal who as, 'I am,' revealed Myself to Moses" (cf. Exodus 3:14). This could also be interpreted as follows; "As God who became man I stand before you, but as God, I am outside time as you experience it; in another time-frame than you, and therefore existed before Abraham". This means that, as the Eternal God, He always just **IS**, while only mankind is moving through time. In His person, as both God and man, He actually attested that time and eternity just is a ***unity***.

In the same way He is also the, "One which **is**, and **was** and **is to come** on the clouds" (cf. Revelations 1:4). Note the sequence: **not** first "**was**", then "**is**", followed by "**coming**", but while it is true that he "was" and is coming, He always just **IS**. Sometimes the term, "The Eternal NOW" (coined by Paul Tillich), is used, meaning that we can neither live in the past nor the future, but are always in the ***ever-moving now***, for we only experience life as, "**now**." This, however, only refers to man. We can point to a "now" in the past, present, or the future, in that when something will happen, we'll say, "***Now*** is the time." God, though, is not ***now, now, now,*** moving through time like we are; He just **IS** the, "I am," and does not move through time or experience it as passing at all. He simply does not live in our sense of time, but **above** and **beyond** it. He is the overruling God of each "now" in our time. In being outside of time, He is, "the high and lofty one, who inhabits eternity" (Isaiah 57:15).

In terms of how we normally observe time, He existed before creation, and even after our history comes to an end, will continue to exist forever. As the Eternal "I AM" and unbound by time, though, He forms and shapes our existence like a glassblower blowing out a big bubble, without getting caught up in it Himself. We may liken Him to a father watching his child on a spinning wheel, and who can make the wheel spin faster or stop, and accompanies the child through all his fears and joys, while Himself standing still. He can also be compared to a **grandfather** who ***immutably*** sits outside on the patio, observing his offspring running around to meet schedules and can see everything happening at a glance, without going through it Himself. He can also be likened to the sun, continuing to shine while giving birth to numerous life-forms and events as they come and go. "God is not in time". It is more correct to say that time is in God. Although there is **logical** succession in his thoughts, there is ***no chronological*** succession" (A. H. Strong). His Being, in wisdom, enters and flows into our time, while blessing or chastising us according to what we are, do and need, in the same way as the sun hardens clay but melts ice.

The difference, of course, is that the sun and earthly fathers are subject to time and grow older, while God, immutably, just **IS**. All of life passes under His eyes, but He ***sits*** on the throne, enjoying the serenity of majesty (cf. Revelations 4:2). He cannot change, grow older or pass through a succession of events (cf. Hebrews 13:8). Nothing can overcome Him and He can suffer no ruin, but is just pulsating Love working out His purpose. To say that He existed **timelessly prior** to creation is thus **not** correct, for this suggests that He is still subject to time, while He did **not** live way back before creation. In fact, all of our existence, time included, expands from Him like a **one-day lily** from a mother plant. His abode is above our experience of time, He is the **ever-present tense** or ***life-giving "Present"***, (the **NOW**), not subject to time cycles at all. We can thus not even talk about a 'time' when time was created, for time as such, does not exist to God. Time, like that lily, buds forth eternally from God; His existence actually **IS** Time, for it flows from Him.

Also, to say that eternality means that He simultaneously is **prior** to creation, at **present**, and already is at the end of time, is merely ***mind-gymnastics***. Neither does our beginning still exist, nor are we already at the end. Some people already are with Him in heaven, but they are no longer in our time. God just is NOW! He is present in every earthly second, acts out His plan in history, in omniscience knows our past and our future, and thus in a single glance sees everything as an ***open book***, and as such, could convey this knowledge to prophets for them to foretell the future. He **IS** eternal life (1 John 5:20), knowing all of history. Which, again, cannot mean that He just from eternity, in the past, had known what was bound to happen, but beholding all from his eternal sphere, He just "**now**" knows what had happened, is happening and will happen? We should also not say time to Him is one ***moment***, for moment as something trivial and fleeting has a bad sound compared to his glory: his ***I AM*** spells fullness of triumphant, fiery life; experiencing all of what happens in the cosmos!

***

The next to note is that **God's eternality** and eternal life in **heaven** also **differs**, for, while He Himself does not experience it as such, heavenly life surely comprises of a *succession of events*, just as they occur here on earth. This is borne out by the fact that angels sing (events), or go out on (sequential) missions to serve people (cf. Hebrews 1:14). This suggests a **sequence of events** or a **rhythm**, otherwise heavenly life would come to a standstill or freeze. When speaking about heavenly time, perhaps it would be better to call it "***timeless perpetuity***", or something along that line. However, in heaven, no ageing or loss can be attached to this concept of time; life in heaven could only be a fullness and completeness of satisfaction. **God** Himself **differs** from this process though, for He does not even experience such an event as perpetual movement, but **is** just the complete and contented God and Giver of life! (from the Greek word "makarios" -happy) (cf. 1 Timothy 1:11).

TIME IS NOT PASSING; WE ARE PASSING AWAY!

However much man has tried, it is impossible to create ***perpetual motion***; a device that can continue to operate on its own using gravity, magnetism, momentum, or whatever. Somewhere along the line it always fails. This failure is due to the Laws of Thermo-dynamics caused by sin, as perpetual motion is only possible in a sphere where **more** energy is available than is **lost** by the operation of the device. And man cannot counteract these laws, as too much energy is always lost. Only God as the source of eternal energy can cause what He creates to function forever.

This also applies to time. The main insight required to fully grasp the concept of time, is to realize that **God did not create time as we**

know it; simply existence in perpetual motion or ***timeless perpetuity***. Time, as **we** recognize it, results from **sin**. This is of extreme importance, for what obscures the correct understanding of time is that, although heavenly and earthly times, as the Bible shows, run **parallel**, they are **experienced** as vastly different. What is **again** overlooked is that we are not just dealing with earthly and heavenly sequences of events, but that time as we now experience it, is not at all the glorious "Present" that God established. It may be true that ***days***, which provide us with a fixed rhythm to go to work, rest at night and worship on the seventh day, were instituted by Him. What we **now** know as ***time***, though, was caused by **SIN**. If we overlook this, we will never understand what is really at play. **Before** man's fall there only was perpetual perfection. The curse following sin: "in the day that thou eatest thereof thou shalt die" (Genesis 2:17), though, instituted earthly life as we **now** know it, causing it to become painful, transient and terminal (coming to an end). From that event time would no longer be experienced as a situation parallel to that which is in heaven, but had become corrupted, **as had man**, immersing life in a restricted framework, ending at death. Before, similar to the unmingled joy of heaven, time was simply a blissful movement through events without any loss of momentum; a ***sequence of beauty*** without negative realities such as decay, pain or loss through aging. Yesterday's beauty was as glorious as today's. It was simply **love** flowing according to God's purpose, without experiencing time different in any way from the love in heaven.

Had they not sinned, Adam and Eve would still have remembered and talked about ***the day*** Abel was born or ***times*** when they shared certain experiences together, but this would not have included any challenging, unprofitable or regrettable times. They would not have grown older, have known what it is to labour, or even that time was passing. Their children would have grown up but not aged or have lost vitality and no-one would have died. It would simply have been ongoing ***development*** according to God's will, in a world enveloped in unblemished love. Sin and the curse on sin, thus resulted in a ***sequence of unpleasant events*** which otherwise would have been unknown. A tarnished past, a worrisome present and a fearful future are all realities shaped by sin, not by God. Earthly life will always be wrapped up in memories of imperfect moments and times falling short of pure love. We will always be ***in time*** for unpleasant events and situations, and ***never too late*** for losses, only late for true bliss. We can gamble away and lose time, miss opportunities, hate every minute because of pain and stress about deadlines for accounts, work and so on. Everything deteriorates, decays, becomes useless and rots. To top it all, time leads to desolation and always takes a most unpleasant turn; **death!** Sin has spawned a dying creation bound to end in total destruction.

The day man sinned, life entered a bizarre, deadly cycle, totally opposed to the heavenly existence. An illegitimate child of infinity was born, "shapen in iniquity; and conceived in sin" (cf. Psalms 51:5); an evil child that shattered love's timeless perpetuity into splintered glass harmful to man. Eternal glory had become vulgar, leading to the promise of injury. Sin caused the collapse of cosmic beauty, in that all of substance, including man's spirit, became harsh and unyielding. Sin thus also led to the ***collapse of eternality***, resulting in the temporality and brokenness we know so well. Shall we call it ***fallen*** or ***continuously falling*** time? What we now Experience as Time, now tarnished by wars, danger and suffering, as opposed to heaven's bliss, though, is merely the ***collapsed state of just perfect and harmonious being!***

"BEFORE THE FOUNDATION OF THE WORLD"?

Another reason why we don't observe life as protruding from God's "NOW" like a bubble from a glassblower's pipe, is that the Bible records events that happened ***before the foundation of the world*** (cf. John 17:24, Ephesians 1:4, 1 Peter 1:20). This creates the impression that time already existed **before** the world was created. This is a misconception, and an explanation of the correct state of affairs hinges on the meaning of the Greek words "**pro**" and "**apo**". (For a more complete explanation of these words and how they affect the teachings on divine election, read "***Die Logos Liefdeskode***").

How it upsets e.g. the Big Bang theory, though, is that when we scrutinize the words ***before the foundation of the world***, some key facts emerge. The most significant is that for the word "before", the Greek word "pro" is used, which does **not** mean long ago before the world existed. Except for ***before*** in time, it has the meaning of, "above," or, that which is superior; as it is used in 1 Pe 4:8, "***above*** (pro) all things have fervent charity." This also is the meaning of "pro" in e.g. Col 1:17, "He (Jesus) is **before** (: superior to) all things, and **by him all things consist**." In line with His words, "before Abraham was, I am," "before" in this case thus does **not** mean, "**prior to**" in time, but rather "**from above**" or "outside" time; from an ***eternal perspective!*** Had He referred to a period prior to Abraham in earthly time, He would have said, "Before Abraham **was**, I **was**." He specifically says, though, that He did **not** live before Abraham in time, but that as the, "I Am," His existence is elevated above our time. He always just is the, "**I am**" from which all proceeds.

"Before the foundation of the world" thus cannot mean **long ago**, but rather, ***from His lofty elevation***. Note that in John 17:5 He prays "glorify thou me with thine own self with the glory which I had with thee **before the world was**." Since earthly time did not yet exist then, the phrase "before the world was", can only mean above time (pro), in our (the Father and Son's) eternality. This is also the meaning conveyed in John 17:24, "thou lovedst me before the foundation of the world." Of course, from **our** point of view on time, the Father loved Jesus **prior** to creation, but as the Eternal, He just loves Him with a boundless, timeless love.

THE MAIN QUESTION!

Our quest is now to show how our time and eternity can still be one. As the fact of Jesus' becoming man and His words show, earth's time is **still** a line running **parallel** to heaven's program. This is important, for, if we, as we tend to, see our time as a sequence of events **separate** from that of heaven, as a line running from far back in an eternal past up to when God created, from then up to now, and from now forward into the future, our own minds already push Him and his acts in creating back to way back when!

Instead, picture a line running from far left to far right, a continuity extending from the original creation to the new heavens and earth. Now see the throne of the Eternal positioned above the line (not back in time), with the line from both ends ***cupped*** between his hands. Now the situation looks different; as Creator he upholds and beholds all earthly time at once, and all of time is governed by the ***Eternal NOW***. Looking up from any point along the line you always will just see Him who was, is and shall come. He does not pass through our sense of time. He is **in** time and time is **in Him**, but He just **IS**. When man sinned, being Love, His love just kept flowing from the eternal sphere into earthly time so as to provide the necessary atonement for sin. As God who became man, He stepped into "***ruined***" time, experiencing temporality, and was thus simultaneously **in** our time **and** eternity, just as He as God was all along, with His people in Egypt and through the desert (cf. Matthew 2:15, 1 Colossians 10:4). Which is why He, while on earth, when speaking to Nicodemus, could refer to Himself as, "the Son of **man** which ***is*** in heaven" (John 3:13).

TIME'S WATERWHEEL!

In order to view time from another angle, let's compare it to a **water wheel** in a river. Though any such comparison will have flaws, it does illustrate what is at play. With all of time still being ***cupped between God's hands***, the water in the stream in which the wheel is placed, flows forever from He who **is** life (cf. John 1:3,4). This is the water of life, clear as crystal, proceeding from His throne (cf. Revelations 22:1). The water (the symbol for ***energy***, as mentioned previously), powers and drives the cosmic wheel, which is ***circular*** because it originates from, and returns to God (cf. Romans 11:36). The wheel differs from the water, but would not have been there was it not for the water. The water itself is unblemished, eternal, and although driving the wheel, does not really pass through the time-cycle of the wheel, which is rusted and decaying. The water does not grow older or lose capacity, but causes the eternal flow of life. Even the water distributed by the wheel is absorbed by the surrounding sand and in the end, filters back into the stream.

If we view history as such a turning water-wheel and people as its buckets, each person is given a chance to complete a cycle from birth to death. On the other hand, we can also see God's timelessness when compared to our sense of time. While His energy drives and upholds the cosmos, the buckets pass through a cycle and each is given a chance to fulfill its purpose. Can you picture a wheel so large as to have **7 billion buckets**, all of them able to procreate and provide new ones to take their place and start their own life-cycles? At the end of each life-cycle, when they reach the bottom of the wheel, they detach and are taken up in the eternal stream. We may even add that some of them only survive a few turns of the wheel, but others 80 or more. Because man is sinful, though, we note that the buckets are dirty and become more corroded, some are even turned upside-down (unbelievers), and in a meaningless existence, don't gather water from the true river of life at all, while as sinners, **all** buckets have holes, causing them to leak.

This means that, although they differ, there is a direct connection between the ***wheel of time*** we know and the waters of eternity which are timeless. ***Cupped*** between His hands the Eternal One upholds all that happens in time; thus observing each moment, the beginning as well as the end. ***In Him*** the water beyond the wheel is already at its destination and He knows what its flow will accomplish in history, as well as each bucket's life. Being Omniscient, He knows the future as if it had already occurred. This is why He could allow John to see believers from all ages already present in heaven (cf. Revelations 7).

As I said, had man not sinned, there would not have been a decaying ***wheel of time***. As in heaven, life would just have been a joyous procession following His purpose, giving man the opportunity for the full use of his potential. There would not have been ageing and death, but just a second, cosmological *stream* of fullness of life parallel to that of heaven. Although we experience it differently, all of what God had established is thus a ***unity***. A unity that engulfs **all** of what He instituted. From the Biblical texts, one can ascertain that, unseen to our eyes, there are different ***levels* of existence** instituted by Him in which God is enthroned as the heart of life (cf. Revelations 4:2). Here we refer to the realm of **heaven**, the physical **universe we** know, and a **dark level** in which Satan and his evil spirits reside. These levels are only *divided* in that they consist of different shades of energy. This can be likened to a globe simultaneously emanating four colors of light that do not interfere with one another. Just as sunlight, oxygen, gravity and electro-magnetism coexist in the same sphere without hindering one another, the waters of life as living energy display different levels of existence exuding from the throne.

Heaven is thus an elevated sphere, and that of evil, a level lower than ours. Although we can only see our level, God, existing timelessly ***above*** and ***just behind*** that which we see, is **in** and pervades all. He is not far from any one of us, "For **in him** we live, and move and have our being" (Acts 17:27,28). The Greek word for "in," is translated as "we are **connected** to, or **surrounded by**, God." Being Omnipresent, He is elevated above the sequence of events both in heaven and on earth while, at the same time, is still present in each tick of our clocks.

THE "NOW"!

These texts again imply that creation simply came about and exists in God's "**NOW**", as demonstrated by the fact that we can only observe the waterwheel (history) in the **present**. Surely this is not easy for us to grasp, as we normally experience time as passing, a series of "**nows**" presented as continuous change. Objects, substances and people deteriorate, age and pass away, a sequence in which nothing is permanent, and each second of pain or happiness differs from all the others. From this experience of time we then conclude that time just is a ***continuous*** course **along which** God created the heavens and earth and which always existed as we now know it. We can see our present understanding of time revealed in our experience of happy families having all they need, and the years just flowing along like a golden dream, until one dies or calamity strikes and they are bereft of all assets. The days then become wearisome nightmares, each second weighs down on them and they count the days in the hope of a change of fortunes. So also, was the pristine state such a golden sequence of events. The fact is, however, that in heaven, time as created by God does **not** pass as if it is lost forever. We only **think** that it does, and don't fully understand or experience the NOW. This feeling of time can thus also be attributed to the ***collapse of timeless glory***.

Had man not sinned, we would have neither experienced events or situations coming to an end, nor suffered any loss. Most important, we would not have even been aware of a time before creation. We would have been like children who don't ask where they were before birth, and only know that they come from their parents who have just always been there. Man would have simply known that life was given to him by God. Before sinning, Adam just accepted that he came from the Eternal, and had he not sinned, this is all that we too, would have known. The fall thus also blacked out all knowledge of perpetual and blissful being. We simply don't know what it is! Blinded by the consequences of sin, we can only think in terms of time as we now know it, and then believe that this experience of time is all that there is, giving rise to ideas of a Big Bang and evolution. This is worsened by the fact that people, because they could not have seen or experienced the true eternal life, due to the anguish of this life, sometimes cannot understand that a **loving** God is the Creator.

Time then, exists for us as an internal screen which hides God's eternality. In Him the only moment in time is NOW, for, although we don't experience it this way, it is only the NOW that exists; although sometimes we may have the lurking feeling that there is more to it. What makes it so difficult to grasp, is that, from our viewpoint, there once was a situation in which God existed while the cosmos had not yet been created. However, this does still not mean that either He or His creation is subject to passing time. This would be similar to you blowing up a balloon and slowly letting the air out, producing a delayed time-sequence in which you, yourself are not involved. God can create as many sequences as He likes, without Himself being subject to time. He exists ***prior*** to creation, not in chronological time, but in the sense of overseeing ***from above!***

The question may also arise as to why He only chose to create at this particular stage, and where He **was**, or what He **did** trillions of years before creation. Even if we accept that the cosmos may be 10 billion years old, the question would still be valid as to why he had not created it **1000 billion** years ago! This is where our concept of time causes confusion, as, in terms of His eternality, He technically could not be said to have created **at any *stage* at all**. He always just **IS**, and creates in the **NOW**. We experience it in terms of time, but, ultimately, that's where we **still** are, in the **NOW**! The question is thus not ***where God was*** before creation, but rather, where we were before birth. We simply were "in the Eternal", as mentioned earlier, "**in His loins**." All living beings whether on earth, in heaven or damnation, still live in the NOW, while the unborn are still in his loins. From his eternality He gave us life, and can also bring new beings into existence so as to also exist in the ***eternal NOW!***

Taste it on your tongue; we don't experience time as NOW because we still think in terms of elapsing and **passing** time, as if it **always** was like this, while in fact, we only live in the NOW and from the Eternal NOW. This is the miracle of NOW; we are only aware here and NOW. Note that **history** can be described, and explained, but it does not really exist. All of those who have died have moved on to a level of ***timeless perpetuity***, while we still experience life as moments of "Now", while those who are yet to be born will also just live in the "now." This can be likened to being in the **spotlight** of a **light-tube** shining from above. Hitler, Napoleon and other historical figures all lived in the "now" of God's light, and so do we. We came "down the tube", were born as part of the ***waterwheel***, and on dying, merely move to a higher level to share in eternality; just as Jesus, who entered our broken time, died on the cross and was taken up to the Father in the eternal NOW. The sinners' concept of time, as a passage of often painful events, resembles the act of ***moving through this light-spot***, while time itself, like a dreadful wind which causes ageing and decay, actually **moves through us.**

Even while we suffer and die one after another, we are still in the NOW, and were it not for man's fall we would have had no problem understanding time at all, but would just have been blissfully happy. At present, however, in the same manner as we are moving through time, time as a curse is moving through us as well. Immersed in **sinner's time**, we are just being ripped apart by ***Father Time's scythe***; cutting, damaging, ageing and humbling us. Only when our corrupted experience of time as born from sin is regenerated with the new heavens and earth, will it again be eternal. The new heavens and earth, after being restored to glory, will just be **perpetual bliss** without the ugly experiences occurring within ***"fallen" time*** and history.

As mentioned previously, this is important as this means that there could not have been a ***time*** **before creation.** An earthly sequence of events only came into existence when our level of being was created, introducing time as we now know it, after the fall of man. Both before and after our earthly lives, though, everything just **IS**, and the "I Am" from whom life emanates, ***cups*** all between his hands. Creation simply extends from the eternal NOW and in the NOW oscillates through time like a child on a swing.

The fact that God cannot be placed in the category of time, but simply IS, further means that He could **not** have decided on divine election or any other event in terms of a time-schedule such as a year or even ten thousand years ago. As the unchangeable, not subject to time, His counsel, immutably, just **IS** who He is. To us this means "always," but to Him as The timeless present tense, it is the NOW. Above and unbound by time, His deeds and eternal decisions just are choices made in the state of "I Am"... the NOW! We may also liken our own life-cycle to a gymnast on the ropes, swinging through time using different techniques, while the ***shackle*** in the roof, that which supports him, is static. Our sense of time is linear, but God, who just **sits** on His throne, is not subject to it; it is only we that are linearly moving with the pendulum. We thus **don't fit into a system** which specifies millions of years before and after creation, **just into God's "I AM".**

It is precisely the view God is the Creator of such a system that also gives rise to the idea that **evolution** is possible. Accepting that all of life flows only from Him, above, with our concept of time directly coupled to heaven and His eternality, means that there **neither** was a time **before** creation, **nor** the passage of billions of years before man came onto the scene. Everything just emanates from the Eternal! As a result, all of creation is given a delightful immediacy. We're living under the eyes of God, who emanates a panorama of light and life which we experience as a sequential existence. **Now**, time and eternity are not in conflict but **ONE**. God is not speaking to us from long ago; we're **now** listening to a living God. The past no longer has meaning and the future does not yet exist; in Him, all just is a unity. In His eternal light we see both the dawn and sunset of history.

Seeing that life is emanated by the eternal "I Am," it also becomes clear that the possibility of **evolution is ruled out**. That there was a time before man's existence during which **development** could have taken place, is just a feeling resulting from man's sin. Moreover, evolution is based on the idea that life-forms have improved with development, while many such forms have actually died out in the process. **As this process**

of suffering and death was caused by the sin of man as the most recent life-form to emerge on the scene, the life-forms which existed during the four billion years before man should have been perfected and also exempt from death. While all it has been shown that all such creatures had a very restricted life span and died, they were clearly not spared. The events relating to sin and the fall only prove again that only the Bible can be true and suffering results from man's sin!

MORE LIGHT SHED ON TIME!

A strong argument used in favor of both evolution and the Big Bang, is that light has a **fixed *travelling speed*** of **300 000 km. per second**. As stars and galaxies start radiating light when they are formed and because we now see them, and it can be approximately determined how far a star is away from earth, they therefore assume that these distant stars and galaxies must be as old as the time it took for their light to reach the earth, which according to their calculations, is millions of years.

Although this sounds like good logic, the argument, once again, does not take into account that the **curse on sin** changed everything. According to the Second law of Thermo Dynamics, because entropy enfolds an irreversible process of disorder, time has a specific ***direction*** and include the processes of decay, ageing and death along the so-called ***arrow of time***. While this law, as stated, directly results from man's **sin**, the next conclusion is that it resulted in a sense of elapsing time, time-frames and time-dilation, as well as **changing the properties of light itself**, and to such an extent that light became something **other than pure *love-energy***. Science is still at its wits end on whether light photons really exist or just are energy-charges, for they can act either as **particles or waves**. Light **is** actually electromagnetic waves, **not** a chemical compound, and has no chemical formula. As we already know, however, all energy can **change** into **matter having a mass,** which is, as we have seen, what happened after the curse on sin.

The point is that in heaven, where the glory of God and the Lamb **is** its light (cf. Revelations 21:23), light surely does not consist of particles in the form of fixed amounts of energy that we call photons. In earth's pristine state light thus differed and did **not** have a certain ***travelling speed***, a limitation which only results from light attaining particle-mass ("weight"). It now actually also has a momentum, such as when you thump a wooden floor so hard that it causes objects to fall from shelves. In other words, light can have an impact on the things on which it shines on and an excess even cause cancer in living beings. This makes it easier to understand that we **cannot deduce the age of earth from the time that it takes for light from stars and other cosmic bodies to reach us**, or even estimate that the cosmos is billions of years old. In the beginning, energy was not limited to any concept of speed, emanating forth according to God's plan, but its composition was changed by the curse! While people presume that this light has taken so long to reach us, according to the Bible the light was always just there, but only acquired mass and a certain ***speed*** since the curse, and the age of the cosmos therefore cannot be derived from such calculations.

MORE LIGHT ON LIGHT!

This also clarifies the question of how, when God created the universe, there already was **light** from **day one**. The period between days one and two is referred to as evening and morning, while the sun, moon and stars were only created on **day four** (cf. Genesis 1:3-16). It is conspicuous that, when darkness is mentioned at the time Jesus was crucified, it is not stated that the sun stopped shining and it became dark, but rather that there was **darkness** and **then** the sun was darkened (cf. Luke 23: 44-45)! We get the same differentiation in Genesis 1; first **darkness**, and **then** God commanded that there should be **light**. This could not have been light from the sun as this was only created on day four. This all means that, like the darkness surrounding the cross, on the first three days of creation, light directly ensued as commanded by God. For example, even when the thick darkness covered **Egypt**, His people had light in their houses (cf. Exodus 10:23). The truth is that He first radiated this light (-energy) **Himself**, and then created heavenly bodies to carry on this task at night; alike "the glory of God shone" around the shepherds (cf. Luke 2:9). This is why Paul was able to say, "For God, who **commanded the light to shine out of darkness**, hath shined in our hearts, to give the light of the knowledge of the glory of God in the face of Jesus Christ" (2 Corinthians 4:6). Light and darkness are thus independent of the sun and the stars. God ***is light*** and can therefore give either outer or inward light or darkness, as and when He wishes (cf. Isaiah 45:7, 1 John 1:5; 4:8), or can also use other means (instruments) to do so, such as the sun.

Note that in the beginning God worked in this way in **all** respects, first performing certain acts Himself and then using ***natural*** processes He had instituted. Dividing the waters below from those above, was counter to the law of gravity, this He simply overruled (or else the law also resulted from the curse!), However, **afterwards** He let this law take a natural course. He **first** created man, plants and animals by Himself, and then allowed them to multiply by **natural** processes, creating the appearance of everything existed by itself. Man, animals and earth were made, **then** man was given dominion to rule over all (cf. Genesis 1:28). So also, **He** gave light, created the days and nights, and on day four made the sun to continue this as a natural process; to "**rule over** day and night, light and darkness" (verse 18). The sun does not create day and night; **He** is the **only Maker**. Just like man, the sun, moon and stars are just His **servants**! This is why it could become dark around the cross, when for a while, the sun died!

Light was thus not, as is sometimes proposed, created ***in-radiation***, that just **makes it *look*** as if it has already been on its way to earth for millions of years. Light-energy came directly from Him. With the words; "let there be light," He simply caused His light to shine through all of space, just as His glorious Being **is** the light of heaven, even where there is no sun or moon (cf. Revelations 21:23).

After the curse light just took on "***photonic clothing***", as all energy had now become harsh and material. Adam also took form using all the available shades of energy, **later** to become **flesh and blood**. While Adam and Eve's children would just have seen them as if they were born that way, they had, in fact, undergone a vast change. So we now see flowers and stars... and think that this is how it originally was and ***was meant to be!***

We tend to first explain everything scientifically, and very soon, Jesus fades away as if only natural laws count. Genesis 1, though, reads; "As the real Light, He is the **giver** of the cosmic marvel!" As John says, "In the beginning was the Word–Jesus; He was **the light of men**... the light **shineth in darkness...**" (cf. John 1:4-9). Everything revolves around

the Light and all goodness we experience is radiated by His glory. Except for the brokenness that has ensued on this earth, that's how it still is!

DISTORTIONS!

If, as previously mentioned, the earth is the center of the universe, it is logical that the negative properties of ***fallen time*** will decrease the further you move away from man and earth. Although in God's eyes all of life just is in the eternal NOW, galaxies and other celestial phenomena, still under the curse, in relation to each other appear to be in different time warps (distortions). As proven by experiments with synchronized clocks, the further away from earth, the less time-elapse occurs! It thus is probable that far out in space practically no time-elapse exists at all, and everything spontaneously flows, more closely resembling God's original plan. This shows that all of creation is affected by earth where the fall actually took place. As a matter of **fact**, the further we move away from **man** as the cause of corrupted time, the less that the negative consequences of the fall can be seen. This applies especially to animals, plants and insects. Animals bring their young into the world with less effort or pain during labour (cf. Genesis 3:16), are less susceptible to sickness, more independent, find it much easier to get food and know what role they should play in their social structures. Our human senses of smell, hearing and eyesight are not as effective as that in some **lower** life-forms from which we are supposed to have evolved. We need a large variety of food types to get proper nutrition, while most of the lower forms' bodies manufacture essential vitamins by themselves. Although no-one teaches insects and birds how to build nests or care for their offspring, all species are highly skilled and proficient at these tasks. It seems that more of their initial giftedness was kept intact than in the case of man. All of this once again reveals the harsh reality of sin and its consequences.

If these truths do not enlighten your mind, it may simply not be working very well.

LAWS?!

According to the logic of physics, the Big Bang itself could neither follow from fixed existing laws, nor have shaped them. Where could these laws possibly have originated then? All the laws of physics which apply to our existence are completely **inexplicable**. Four powers in nature **must** remain constant so as to ensure order: electro-magnetism, gravity and weak and strong nuclear forces. Had the "strong" power binding sub-atomic particles in our bodies been just a little stronger, their influence on one another would have caused major problems for us. Had they been a little weaker, the universe would only have consisted of hydrogen and the whole physical system as we know it, would have been doomed (cf. Alberts, 1997). The same holds more or less true for **all** of nature's forces. Not only can **no-one** explain **what** these forces are, but they cannot (especially not evolutionists), inform us why they are exactly in place as to ensure our orderly existence.

For example, the moon keeps its place in space because of the precise delicate balance between its trajectory speed and earth's gravity. Were it not for the pull of gravity holding it back, it would have moved away from the earth. Were its speed too slow, gravity would have pulled it in and it would have already smashed into earth. Should it move faster, centrifugal force will also cause it to move away. The pull of the gravity of the earth **exactly balances** with the trajectory speed of the moon. Should planetary speeds slow down or their gravity increase, **all** heavenly bodies will be drawn towards each other and horrific smashes will result! **No-one** can explain what keeps these powers in balance; yet each planet, star or comet has exactly the **right speed within its gravitational field.** Laws like this result in the universe as a whole functioning smoothly. They establish the behavior of energy, how electrical charges influence each other, and govern thermodynamics and other processes.

The point is that these laws could **only** have originated by intelligent design, not at all on their own, as the fact that they exist at all, **prevents** chaos and create stability. They clearly did not devise the cosmos, for laws cannot create, only bring order. If not given by God, how could they have existed before anything else did? Moreover, these laws do not depend on each other, they differ widely, but still work in harmony to keep life in shape, each of them of equal importance so as to allow everything to co-exist and to make life possible.

This means that the universe must have been created with **all** natural laws in place, otherwise it would not have functioned as it does, as proven by the perfect order and beauty that we see. **Each** facet of life sings of perfect planning and control. Approximately seventy factors have to be in harmony to make the earth livable for all life forms. These factors have already been identified (Ross and Hayward, 1989; The Logos Code, 2011). Had each law developed on its own, how could there be such unity without them counteracting each other. If gravity, for instance, affected nuclear forces, this would have resulted in chaos. Order can only come from a power that built all laws into the system from the beginning, so as to supplement one another and direct life (cf. Alberts, 1997).

8. THE EARTH IS YOUNG!

All of what we have shared up to now points to the fact that the earth **cannot** be as old as 15 billion years as argued by evolutionists, and that their theory is thus impossible. This becomes more evident when we examine radiometric tests in the light of the great flood in Noah's time and the genealogical evidence given in the Bible.

RADIOMETRIC TESTS!

As a term, ***radiometric tests*** may sound high-minded, but they are not that difficult to understand. To establish when animals and man first appeared and how they succeeded each other, these tests are used on the petrified remains (fossils) of plants, people and animals that have died and are found in earth's geological formations. The results are then used to put together an ***almanac*** of history (the geological timetable), which informs us how old are various objects. These tests are thus an important witness to confirm the possibility of the Big Bang and the theory of evolution, the belief that everything developed over a very long period of time. This long time span which they indicate is also the reason why many **Christians** feel that the ***six days*** of Genesis 1 should be seen as periods of millions of years.

Our **only** question is whether these tests are **valid** at all, as we contend that they are **not**! In short, we can liken this problem to someone receiving a gift of a **thousand white marbles** in a box, and on every birthday exchanges one with a **black** one. Later in life his age can then be deduced from the number of black marbles in the box. More or less the same reasoning is applied in this case to determine the age of things; because it is given as a fact that, as time passes, a loss of electrons takes place, resulting in elements decaying and **forming other elements.** As mentioned previously, elements only differ with regard to the number of protons, neutrons and electrons present in their atoms. This can vary depending on the addition or subtraction of these sub-atomic particles. This means that when electrons are lost due to decay or other factors, the **element itself changes into another element**. Uranium decays to thorium and then lead; carbon-14 decays to carbon-12, and so on. Because the tempo of decay remains the same (as in one *marble* per year), radiometric tests are then based on the amount of the **new** element that has formed (e.g. the lead in petrified bones), and scientists can then deduce how much time has elapsed for it to have reached that level, and thus how old is the substance, fossil or object.

The problem is that many scientists agree that these tests are ***not reliable*** for various reasons. For example, they would be based on the assumption that **no lead** was present in a stone when it was formed, and if there was, the test will be of no value. As in the case of our example, no-one can tell how many **black marbles were already** in the box at the time that the counting started, or whether there were any black marbles originally present at all, as no-one bothered to check the box all those years ago! Furthermore, either the uranium or the lead could have diminished or increased as a result of **other** factors, such as when someone else placed black marbles into the box.

It is also possible that such elements, under certain conditions, could have been **transferred** to the rock under investigation. Even worse; the rate of decay would have to stay fixed, but certain circumstances can also alter this situation!

Examples exposing the problem are the cases of ages of 3.5 million years being ascribed to three lava sites in New Zealand, which everyone knew were formed as recently as 1950-1975. **Argon** (a gas) caught up in the lava during the cooling process, simply resulted in the tests showing that these flows were very old. The shells of **still-living** molluscs have also shown an age of 2300 years, and **freshly slaughtered** seals, 1300 years, while some that were frozen for only 30 years, when tested, pointed to ages of 4600 years and more. Tests on basalt rocks in Hawaii, formed two hundred years ago, show an age of 160 million to 3 billion years. On the other hand, carbon tests on fossils that, according to the fossil record should be **350 million** years old, have shown an age of only **4000 years.**

Most people **think** that radioactive dating has proven that the earth is billions of years old, but **it has not.** We may again argue that this is **not the fault of science,** as the technique itself is reliable and scientists can only work with that which is actually present and testable, and that may indeed show apparently very advanced ages for certain objects. While some factors influencing the estimated age of artifacts could be overlooked, sceptics of the Bible, however, **cannot** use these findings to prove the Bible wrong.

What is again Important, is that the appearance of things being linked to **age** is a false assumption which overlooks the effects of **sin**! **The decay used in radiometric tests results from the curse on sin,** which (decay) **began** only **after** the total change involving all of energy/ matter. **This** great truth **wipes evolution from the map!**

THE GREAT FLOOD!

This truth is all the more emphasized by the fact that, just as we could not have seen earth and man as created by God in its pristine state, we can also not see what earth was like **before the flood** and what **changes** it brought about! (most of what was said on the matter in "***The Logos Code***" is repeated here). Apart from the consequences of the curse, a **second** disastrous event took place that changed the world and caused it to appear more ancient than it really is. Once again, the issue of **sin** has been overlooked. As written in Genesis 6:5-7, men became so wicked that it grieved God's heart that He had made them. The flood then ensued as punishment. Note that Peter not only says that, by the word of God the world was created ***from and by water***, he also adds that by the same word of God, "the world that then was, was overflowed with **water** and perished" (2 Peter 3:5,6).

To picture this and how it had led to earth's present appearance with its mountains, coal, oil, fossils and geology, is rather simple. When you squirt water into the ground with a hose, the water displaces small pebbles and sand, whilst the larger rocks are less affected. Grass and sticks remain adrift or get caught up and buried. At the same time, lighter and heavier particles are exposed, covering each other in layers.

Move the hose a little, and you will see whirlpools, again disrupting it all so as to form new layers.

About 30 indicators of such a cataclysmic water event to have struck the earth have already been discovered. Evidence suggests that the water level rose to seven meters above the mountains and covered everything (cf. Genesis 7:20). Remember that they were **not** the mountains as seen today. Many present mountains actually result from the flood, whilst those created earlier could have been much lower. Earth had become a roaring ocean. The change in pressure on its continental plates, which rested on lava, became so vast that they were disrupted. Under water, heavy material has the same weight as the water it replaces and moves fast. This results in the single continent then existing (***Gondwana***, or ***Pangaea***, as is generally accepted), being torn into large slabs, at places pressing up against other plates to form mountains, or sliding over one another. In the process, water streams over the slabs. Massive waves and torrents break the ice at the poles and carry it along. Mighty rivers loaded with rock result in huge ravines being formed. Indications of water moving at very high speeds have been found in many, now dry, places on earth. As a result of the streaming masses of rocky mud under water, helped along by large whirlpools, giant forests, all the inhabitants of the earth and the animals are covered by soil, later to petrify or be converted into oil, gas, or coal. Dead bodies are spread out, laid down and covered in layers of mud.

It has been recorded that during volcanic eruptions, ravines of 200 meters deep were torn away by streams of mud. An eruption in Washington (USA) in 1980 sent a flood wave of **300 meters high** right across Lake Spirit and dumped a **million trees** into the water. Some were buried in mud while others stayed adrift; roots downward. This indicates that situations ascribed to events supposedly occurring long ago, could actually have come about **very rapidly**. The evidence is there for every eye to see. All over the world, clear layers can be observed on the face of mountains where the rock has lifted along breaks.

When the earth's crust came to rest again, vast lakes could now be seen, but some of them flowed in mighty streams to low-lying areas again. Fissures like Meiringspoort (RSA) and the Grand Canyon (USA), come into being. Everything came to rest in new positions. New mountains, lakes and coastlines appeared. Earth's face has totally changed! (The original Garden of Eden will thus never be found). Plants, trees and seeds that stayed adrift took root or germinated again. Life had begun all over. **And... everything is there to later keep miners, archaeologists and oil drills busy.**

Also consider the following: Marine fish can stay alive in fresh water for a long time. There is evidence that coal, oil and diamonds can actually form very quickly, as opposed to millions of years. Coal is found in ***sediment*** caused by water and many fossils of water animals are found in the coal. Experiments have also shown that wood, contrary to earlier research which suggests millions of years, can actually petrify within a few years (Akahane and others). There is proof that mountains at one stage were under water, for example, the fossils of shells and water animals found in mountain peaks such as the Himalayas and other places, which could clearly not have been covered by water for reasons other than a great flood. Herbivorous animals have been found at the poles, frozen in ice. Between large stretches of animal fossils, which are already proof of a sudden water-death, often no grass is found.

The layers in which fossils of dinosaurs are found in Mongolia and the Coconino sandstone and Morrison formations in the USA are examples. Also, several fossils of whales have already been found in deserts and mountains very far from any ocean!

Between the layers in the Grand Canyon there are ***no time-gaps*** or indications that one layer is older than the next. All were laid down in one simultaneous event. The largest part of the earth's crust consists of **sediment** (silt) that was deposited **by water** and hardened, and fossils are often found very **deep** in this sediment. This shows that they were buried very quickly in one massive event. It is **important** to note that fossils **only** form in flood situations and not when a body remains exposed or in a shallow grave. It has to be completely buried, **eliminating all oxygen**; otherwise it will not petrify, but **rot!**

If the layers of ground containing fossils were caused by the flood, then clearly the reason that some similar life-forms still exist today, while others have completely vanished, is that most of the life-forms that existed at that time were caught up in it. Dead material resulting from man's fall, as well as everything that was still alive at the time of the flood, was destroyed and buried during this disaster, and not millions of years earlier as maintained by the evolutionists. It is also during the flood that the **dinosaurs** must have been wiped out, and not by a meteorite striking the earth, as is alleged!

From a scientific perspective it can also be argued that the flood itself, combined with factors such as the immense pressure caused, and changes in radiation, would affect the evidence on which the results of radiometric tests are based, in a similar manner to cooking changing the texture of meat. This means that the great ages attributed to fossils are the result of the flood and that earth is much younger than is believed! Together with a change in the oxygen content of the atmosphere, this could also have resulted in people growing much older before the time of the flood (cf. Genesis 5:3-30: Adam, 930 years, Methuselah, 969 years and so on. The earth looks old, but we believe it only because we have heard this repeated over and over since childhood, and can no longer see the "face" it had when it was created. This is also why it **looks** as if no conclusions about its age can be reached from what the Bible says and history is then deduced from the results of radiometric tests.

The false appearance of the age of the earth simply proves what God said about the flood! The reason why people eagerly accept the advanced age of the world is that, if the flood **did** take place and the earth's history is relatively recent, scientific **time-tables as well as the theory of evolution would collapse!**

GENEALOGICAL TABLES!

From childhood, we have simply accepted it as true that evolutionary development took place over billions of years. In fact, **no-one can really prove it** and **all evidence actually points against it**. Let's face it, all those drawings of hoary men with cudgels living in caves, as seen in books, have taken hold of our minds, but are simply figments of the imagination. There is **no** proof that everything is that old or that the cosmos has developed over millions of years. More than 100 cases of proof of the earth being much younger have already been listed.

If we then consider that archaeology and history also are **sciences**, and neither of them can supply a better explanation of man's past than the Bible, we can view history in a new light. **No other records** of earth's history exist which can provide us with genealogical tables reaching back to the first man, other than that given in Genesis, which shows a record of **10 000** years at the most. The first form of writing came into use in 3100 BC in Mesopotamia, in 3000 BC in Egypt, in 2200 BC in the Indus Valley and in 1300 BC in China. Before that, the history of events was passed on to new generations by means of oral tradition only. No other writings in structured language can thus be much older than the books of Moses. Of all religious texts, the Bible goes back the furthest, with Hinduism second, and traces of it cannot be found further back than 2000 BC. Gautama, the founder of Buddhism, was born in 560 BC and Mohammed in 570 AD. One may ask; **if man has been on the scene for 500 thousand years... why is this development taking place only at such a very late stage?**

The genealogical tables given in the Bible are the only source providing a trustworthy account of what happened all those thousands of years ago, backdating and covering all of history from Adam; portraying a very young earth. Concerning the time from Adam to Christ, we find records in Matthew 1:1-17 and Luke 3:23-38. The time that is most in doubt, is that from Adam to Abraham, but that lineage was carefully recorded in two more places: Genesis 5 and 11, both providing the succession of generations, each time giving the name of the father, his eldest child, and his age when the child was born. This makes it obvious that from Adam to Seth 130 years elapsed (Genesis 5:3), that Enos, Cainan, Mahalaleel, Jared, Enoch, Methuselah, Lamech and Noah followed after him, and that the time from Adam to Noah was 1056 years, and from then on to the flood 600 years passed (cf. 7: 6). The flood can, thus, be placed at 1656 years after Adam.

When Noah was 500, he became the father of Shem, Ham, and Japheth (cf. 5:32). Shem thus was 100 at the time of the flood, and became the father of Arphaxad two years later (cf. 11:10), who at 35 became the father of Salah. (Luke adds Cainan between the two; perhaps another son of Arphaxad? Cf. 3:36). After that, again with the father's age given at each child's birth, we read the names of Eber, Peleg., Reu, Serug, Nahor, Terah and Abram; born 1946 years after Adam (see Genesis 11:13-27).

The total time span thus appears to be: from Adam to Abraham, **1946** years, and from Abraham to Christ, **1900**; giving us a total of about **4000**. If we add **2000** from Christ to today, it brings the total age of the earth to **six thousand years.** This course of events is also supported by the New Testament, showing that Genesis 5 and 11 were still regarded as valid during the time after Christ (cf. Adam: Romans 5:14; 1 Tim 2:13; Cain and Abel: Hebrews 11:4; Seth: Luke 3:38; Enoch: Luke 3:37, Hebrews 11:5; Noah: Matthew 24:37, Hebrews 11:7, 1 Peter 3:20). Jude in his letter counts Enoch as "seventh from Adam" (cf. 14), **just as** Genesis 4:17–5:18 presents it!

The idea exists that the origin of other nations or groups goes back further than that of Israel, but **experts** in this field place the origins of China, Egypt and India, for example, at 3500 BC. This underlines what the Bible recorded about the scattering of nations, as well as that which is said about Israel, fits the picture perfectly. The period when the oldest dynasty of kings ruled Egypt, is fixed by Egyptologists at no more than 3000 BC. According to Genesis 10:6, the Egyptians are descendants of Ham, born when Noah was 500 (cf. Genesis 5:32). His descendants, thus, were one of the tribes from whom "the nations were divided on earth after the flood" (cf. Genesis 10:32).

According to this, his tribe must have grown for 400 years, from 1656 BC, after Adam, up to the Egyptians at the time of Moses (about 1300 BC). Whether the pyramids were built before or after this time, or whether the Israelites helped with their construction, is not stated. Philo (historian), though, recorded that some of them were built with bricks of a mixture of clay and straw and baked in the sun (the material used by the Israelites (Cf. Exodus 5:7). **Compare this with what could have happened to Ham's family in Egypt during the 400 years from 1656-1300 BC (a time which included the building of the pyramids), with the events during the 500 years since America was discovered by Columbus in 1498 (immense cities, computers and space travels included)!**

Information from the Bible is often regarded as blatantly false. God, however, clearly provides a complete view of history which is meant to be taken seriously. We may consider it as strange that He created this wondrous cosmos to only have existed for ten thousand years. It would, however, be even stranger if He had created it to hang around in the sky for 15 thousand million years without anyone around to appreciate it. It is also strange that if people were illiterate for hundreds of thousands of years, to simply proceed, in **just 5** thousand years, from the invention of writing to computers and space travel.

The **only** reason for clinging to the idea of millions of years for earth's history is to wish to reconcile this to evolution's timetable and to refute the Bible. The further God can be shifted back- and outwards, the better it suits evolutionists. Talking about 15 thousand million years ago moves Him far away into oblivion, while if the earth is only six or seven thousand years old, God and His word become a living reality and evolution is clearly impossible.

A CLASH?

Sceptics of the idea of God upholding the universe may point out that such a process clashes with the Second Law of Thermodynamics which states that everything is running down. As is often remarked: if He controls the universe, why does He not eliminate decay, anguish and pain? It just continues, where is His presence then? They also ask if the idea of orderly progress as the result of God's sustaining activity does not also clash with the **first** law, which states that energy **cannot be added** to a closed system, as sustaining, upholding or being otherwise involved indeed means that He is exerting energy on the system.

Of course, there **cannot** be a clash, for God Himself is in control of all laws. The simple answer is that He can both **uphold** everything by the power of His word, while **also** applying the **effects of the curse** (cf. Hebrews 1:3, Matthew 6:19). In other words, the punishment of wickedness continues, so that, **together with** orderly progress, we also find corruption and decay. The "brokenness" of the world proves that which is read in the Bible regarding His righteousness: a cursed earth with anguish, as well as order, so that chaos won't rule. "Heavens and the earth, by the word are **kept in store**, reserved unto fire against the Day of Judgment" (cf. 2 Peter 3:7).

In truth, the laws of Thermo-dynamics confirm that the cosmos is **not a closed system at all**, in that it is sustained by an external power. The reason for this is that, as mentioned earlier, in any system energy only diminishes, as in batteries, vitality in the body and so on. On a macro-systems level, everything is running down like a battery; the cosmos is running out of useable fuel, and slowly dying a heat-death. Had it truly existed by itself for 15 billion years, it would **already** have been **bankrupt** of energy long ago. The evolutionist view that everything, by continuing to develop, is still improving in an upward spiral, is in contradiction with this second law of thermodynamics, and therefore impossible. This means that without external sustenance, all of life would already have been wiped out long ago. This sustenance is proven by the order and beauty present in creation.

If, on the other hand, creation is not that old, and we accept the Biblical calculation of only seven thousand years, we, of course, have a totally different picture. Evolutionists, indeed, do not maintain that the cosmos as a **whole** is improving. They even admit that there is a decline in total energy. A part of the cosmos, such as the earth, though, obtains enough energy from the sun to enable life and progress. Had the cosmos existed for 15 billion years, however, it would have long ago been **depleted** of useable energy. Within this total time frame, the continuation of life, and evolution itself, would thus have been **impossible!**

Furthermore, in the light of the ***Uncertainty Principle***, as termed by science, the unpredictability of the behaviour of each single particle of which reality is comprised, would also have also been a problem without guidance and control. The fact that they seen to act randomly, makes it obvious that, **if not governed and controlled**, everything would have scattered into chaos long ago! The whole universe is thus clearly subject to a magnificent control which reveals purpose, without which life simply would have been impossible: "He upholds all things by the word of his power" (cf. Hebrews 1:2,3). In this case, "upholding" means to prevent something from falling, and to be able to apply it as one wishes.

The fact that disease and wounds can heal, even without medicine, also is a wonder **contrary** to the idea of spontaneous development. Tissue regenerates, skin grows back and bones mend. Although everything does not develop towards perfection as the evolutionists maintain, we do find that brokenness can heal. Is this merely another process that has developed on its own?

The question is therefore why then does this not happen **all** the time? Sometimes the strong do die. The answer is that we still suffer under the **curse** on sin, but, in being loving and tolerant, God does not immediately fully punish people, giving them time to return to Him, otherwise all unsaved persons would have already been lost. Though by his (Jesus') wounds healing came (cf. Isaiah 53:5), even believers don't always experience healing when they want it. God uses suffering as a method of "forming" His people (cf. Psalms 73:1-14). So what is seen all over the world is simply ***perfectly controlled chaos!*** To argue as if the negative events in life are merely ***chance*** and that we have a right to an idyllic life, is, however, to evade the issue.

A last remark in this regard is that, other than what was said in "***The Logos Code***", that only the second law of Thermo Dynamics results from man's fall, they all three, in fact, result from the "***collapse of glory***" and would not have existed without man's sin. Only the **Zeroth** (basis) law, which states that everything always flows from a higher to a lower level, would have originally applied. Had man not sinned, life indeed would have been without entropy, because everything flows from God and the cosmos would have progressed under ideal conditions. The Three

Laws of Thermo-dynamics could thus legitimately be called ***the laws of the cosmos resulting from man's shame of corrupting and introducing the rot into that which was originally bliss!***

9. ENERGY, TWO TREES AND A WORLD OF KNOWLEDGE!

Never in history was there a time when people were so set on gaining knowledge as the present. Just note the focus on information-technology, talk-shows, books and pamphlets; on science, health, nutrition and other areas. Yet man is still searching for the elusive ***Holy Grail*** of happiness while anxiety and uncertainty abound more than ever! The thirst for knowledge just proves that it is something that we've **lost**, and we need help from outside of ourselves. We cannot live without being revitalized, and also in this, scientific knowledge of both bodily and spiritual nutrition agrees with the Bible. The **Holy Grail** means just having **the right food!**

From the beginning, eating was clearly an important part of the "**feast**" that life **was meant to be**. Man was created to be daily **replenished** with energy and the channels to provide this were originally part of creation (cf. Genesis 1:29). This way, man would be kept dependent upon God as the only Giver of life. Work and the use of energy does not result from sin; it was man's love-calling all along (cf. Genesis 2:15); only the tiring aspect of work, and eating in sorrow and tribulation, would prevent its positive outcome. In Genesis 2:9-16, however, we read that there were always **two choices** for man: in the **middle** of Eden stood two trees; the **tree of life** from which, like all the others, they were allowed to eat freely, and that of the **knowledge of good and evil**, which was forbidden. They were told that, should they eat from it, they would die that day. While God did not spell out the importance of the fruit from these trees, we have to deduce this from what He did say, and from what resulted from eating the fruit of the wrong tree.

The key to true understanding is therefore that GOD, as the only Giver of life, asks **humble submission**. All the trees supplied life-sustaining energy, but eating from the forbidden one would mean rejecting Him and the loss of pure energy. Differing slightly from what was said in "The Logos Code" (that man, in the beginning, needed **separate** kinds of food for body and spirit), it now seems more likely that, while it is **not** specifically mentioned, that fruit of the tree of the knowledge of good and evil **differed** from that of the tree of life, the tree of knowledge of good and evil stood apart, opposed to all others. In other words, by **not** eating from it, they were acknowledging the will of God. The other trees supplied energy, but between these two they had to **choose** either submission to, or turning away from God; thus indicating their obedience and sense of responsibility.

The fact that they indeed ate from the forbidden tree and thus obtained the "knowledge of good and evil," means that they knew very well what "**good**" was, for, from the rising sun to what the tongue tasted, all of creation was **good**. They just ***did not know that they knew*** it, simply because one cannot value sweetness without first having tasted bitter. In His omniscience God knew what evil and its consequences enfolded. Man, though, unable to see the ***other side of the***

coin, could only discover this by **doing** evil and **becoming** it! In sinning they thus acquired ***knowledge*** of the **bitterness** of evil as opposed to the sweetness of being good. (To ***know*** is to be intimately acquainted with; cf. Genesis 4:1: "Adam ***knew*** Eve, and she conceived"). Sinning made them ***knowers*** of sin and its dark results! Satan's lie was to insinuate that God did not really love them, and on eating from the forbidden tree, they would become like Him and be better off on their own. However, when man thinks he can be like God he becomes more like Satan; in opposition to God.

The question now is how we can regain true life? What is the right tree? It is important to note that man, after sinning, was driven from paradise so they could not again, "take of the tree of life and eat and live forever" (cf. Genesis 3: 22). In eating from the wrong tree, true life had died in them, and they became "**dead**" in terms of the life of God (living, but dead; cf. Ephesians 2:1-2). Eating from the tree of life would thus have energized them so as to **live forever**, but in their ***fallen*** state. This shows just how powerful are God's means of sustenance. Eating from the forbidden tree before the fall was not required to secure a life free from death; they **were** free and only became subject to it by sinning. Had they eaten from it a second time though, their evil, fallen state would have been fixed, like run-away children living by using their father's bank code.

This may sound fair enough, for this is what unbelievers do, as worldly things are all they want, but Adam and Eve would certainly **NOT** have had the pleasant life that unbelievers often have. However, as the price for their sin has also been paid on the cross, God in forbearance, gives them time to return to Him before the final judgment (cf. 2 Peter 3:9, Psalms 73). If he had eaten from the tree of life again, though, Adam and his progeny would have had **powerful life-support**, but life would still have been **hell** on earth, still subject to the curse of brokenness; **never dying and yet always dying**, existing in anguish without any hope of salvation. Being banned from paradise was already a **mercy**, but man now needed a new way of spiritual energizing based on forgiveness, and finding a way of regaining true life by returning to God's loving arms.

God now instituted a new way of feeding; a change difficult to describe, for as a body-spirit man changed from being angel-like to that which we now know. From that time, the **body and spirit** were sustained in **different** ways. Before the fall, perfect in knowledge of, and love for God, they were vitalized by **fruit** that, as with all of creation, consisted of pure love-energy. While all energy, also fruit, was **now corrupted**, it could only feed the **body** that was of the same corrupted nature, but fruit was no longer appropriate for the spirit, for **God won't feed man's spirit with corrupted energy.** From that time onwards, man's spirit could only be vitalized by **God's** Spirit. In the now-corrected relationship with God, both can, once again, live from both now live from new nuances of energy than in the beginning.

THE NAKED SCIENTIST IN ALL OF US!

Before examining the present way of energizing, let's note that we are all standing ***naked*** before God. Ever since Adam and Eve, nakedness was a symbol of sin (cf. Exodus 32:25, Ezekiel 23:29, 2 Colossians 5:3, Revelations 3:17). Don't we all know the shame of spiritual nakedness when our dishonesty, adultery, jealousy, hatred and other inadequacies are uncovered, or when our conscience drives us up the walls! We now need real clothing, without which we will stay under God's wrath, feeling insecure and wanting! The problem is that we don't easily see that this situation is caused by still eating from the ***wrong tree*** and not the true spiritual food that God now provides.

To once again be clothed in the love of God without feeling any disgrace or need, we should just carefully observe how **He** addressed the problem. Because He is holy, He could not clothe them before sin was confessed and forgiven. Adam's, "I did eat," was a full confession (cf. Genesis 3:12,13). As righteousness demands though, there was also a price to be paid for sin. Adam and Eve, being terrified, tried to cover their disgrace by making themselves aprons from leaves. This could, however, **not** repair their ruin **or** prevent God's wrath. It is beautiful though, that as a sign that He still loved them and wanted them to feel nurtured, God Himself made them clothes to cover their nakedness.

This event goes very deep, however, for it demanded the **first blood** to flow: "Without shedding of blood is no remission of sin (cf. Hebrews 9:7,18,22). Sin deserves death. It had not only turned man into flesh and blood, but all of life into blood, war and agony, and all of creation groaning in pain (cf. Romans 8:22). The first blood, though, flowed when God showed his love towards sinners in the first offering, symbolizing **a life sacrificed for life**. While death was not part of His original creation, and all living creatures were originally given fruit and plants as food, **not meat**, making clothes from skin meant that God had to kill an animal(s) Himself. Just imagine how it made Adam and Eve feel, to see for the first time, the horror of death in the eyes of a living being, and the red blood flowing away, knowing that their sin had caused it.

Furthermore, because an animal's blood is inferior to that of man, it "is impossible for the blood of bulls to take away sins" (Hebrews 10:4). A worthy offering could only be brought by a **man**, and a **perfect man** as such, for one in debt cannot pay others' debts. Moreover, the sacrifice must have the power to cover the debt of **all** mankind, which an animal cannot do! Offerings thus instituted by God in the Old Testament were merely the ***"shadows" of things to come*** (cf. Hebrews 10:1). In other words, the only perfect offering would be the sacrifice of **One** having the power to cleanse all, and this would be brought about on the cross. The Old Testament offerings were thus merely a symbolic payment and forgiveness, in that the Lamb slaughtered later would Himself pay the price that was required (cf. Revelations 13:8)!

God thus covered their shame as to make them feel outwardly acceptable, while inwardly, as a result of the coming sacrifice, they were already fully **clothed in His eyes.**

Although life would now be hard, they could feel cared for. So, in this way, He also brings dead souls back to life: "you, being dead in your sins, hath he **quickened... having forgiven** you all trespasses" (Colossians 2:13). On accepting the clothes gathered from the offering, they were revitalized, or **reborn to life.** Pure love-energy from God restored them as His children. While sin kills real life, forgiveness restores it, so one can again joyously live from and for Him.

This event again points to the unity of body and spirit. Clothing them removed their feelings of guilt, as they felt covered, **and** their spiritual peace, in spite of life's challenges, was restored. It is striking to notice that **the very clothes covering their nakedness was proof that blood had flown to clothe them in grace**; a grace given by God in order to return them to His loving arms, quiet their consciences and change their feelings of insecurity to that of confidence (cf. Hebrews 10:2).

KNOWLEDGE!

Observe that, because man had lost true knowledge as the result of sin, **knowledge** now remains as the **most crucial issue in our lives.** All that which we've said so far, boils down to the fact that we now only search for knowledge so as to **improve** on our **fallen** state, or to fight depravity. The word "**science**" itself comes from the Latin "Scientia", which simply means "**knowledge**," that which encompasses **all** of life. All knowledge can be categorised as science, whether research and experiments can prove the facts presented or not.

Man's problem is that, like Eve, he still thinks there is something better than that which God provides and that his own devices will suffice. In other words, that he can survive on knowledge other than that obtained from living closely to, and from, God.

In a similar manner, Satan deceived Eve. He also tried to tempt Jesus into putting worldly riches, pleasure and food before God. Jesus, though, answered: "Man shall not live by bread alone, but by every word of God" (Luke 4:4,5), and in a similar fashion, He taught His people: "Man doth **not** live by **bread only**, but by every word that proceedeth out of His mouth" (Deuteronomy 8:3). In the Old Testament God made His people initially go hungry and then supernaturally fed them with manna from heaven, so as to teach them that man **only** and directly lives from Him. Natural and spiritual food have the **same origin**, for, as the **Bread of life**, at the **command** from **His** mouth, He gives life in total, while disobeying Him results in sorrow for both body and spirit.

This is also modern man's problem. As man ate fruit from the tree of knowledge thinking that a promised insight was better than that which God provided, fallen man now puts his trust in power, medicine, false gods, philosophies and even convictions that being baptized or performing good works saves him... **all in all, in knowledge itself;** as if this can cure spiritual hunger, secure life or safeguard against his wrath! God indeed uses some of these processes, but to believe that man can provide for himself is to be trapped by the same deception to which Eve succumbed, choosing against Him and becoming His enemy. Moreover, this does not solve the problem. While only God gives life, thinking that life can be sustained by **any other** source than God, is tantamount to eating from the **wrong tree**.

Also, the search for wealth or fame stems from the fact that people feel naked, insecure and seek covering, while false teachings keep them under the pretence that they are on the right track. Under the deception that man can make it on his own, the true Bread of life or the words from His mouth are replaced with spiritual food of one's own choice; which is still from the **same tree of evil** functioning in mans' heart, and he wears a cover of leaves that bring a false feeling of security. Knowledge without acknowledging God is evil and cannot energize man or provide true wisdom and love. The theory of **Evolution**, as a teaching that eliminates God from the picture is thus just a part of Satan's fraud; providing as little comfort as knowing that the oceans are filled with water.

"FOOD THAT ENDURES"

Although the cross on which they hung Jesus is sometimes also called a ***tree*** (cf. Deuteronomy 21: 23, Acts 5: 30, Galatians 3:13), it is

not the *tree of life*. By the fact that He gave his life and shed his blood, Jesus, as Giver of life is Himself the tree of life, in fact, of **eternal** life, while He feeds us by our benefitting from the "fruit" of His sufferings (cf. John 3:16). As a family lives off the fruit of a father's work, we live from the fruit of His suffering; our sins being covered by his blood (cf. John 1:1-3, 1 Peter 1:19). Thus clothed in His blood, God sees us as spotless in His eyes (cf. Hebrews 9:14); as if sinless (cf. Romans 5:1): clothed with the garments of salvation, covered with the robe of righteousness (cf. Isaiah 61:10).

As we've seen, Adam and Eve could not once again eat from any of the two trees; neither from the tree of knowledge, for that entailed a separation from God, nor from the tree of life, for that would have only further sustained the corruption that had followed. They now had to live **by faith alone** while God fed them spiritually. So are **we** also energized by the true source of life. We live from Jesus both in body and spirit as "the **true bread** from heaven" that meets all our needs (cf. John 6:32), and from the words of His mouth. Which is why He says: "Do not work for the ***food that perishes***, but for the ***food that endures*** to eternal life, which the Son of Man will give to you" (John 6:27. ESV). Strive to know God better and to trust Him.

Interestingly, from the earliest times God has forbidden the eating of blood because, "the **life** of the flesh is **in the blood**" (Leviticus 17:10,11). This is accurately demonstrated by the fact that, when the blood flows out, life drains away and one dies. By forbidding the eating of it, God taught us **respect** for life. Jesus, though, says "**Unless** you eat the flesh of the Son of Man and drink his blood, you have no life in you" (cf. John 6:50-53). Why did He say this? This is actually an analogy. For example, when David said that his enemies wanted to eat his flesh, he meant that they wanted to profit from his death (cf. Psalms 27:2). Jesus is thus indicating that, by having faith, we **benefit from his death.** David also spoke of **drinking the blood** of others. After his enemies overran Bethlehem, David remarked how much he would love a drink from its well. On hearing it, brave soldiers fought their way through, drew water from the well and brought it to him. He then said, "Far be it from me that I should **drink the blood** of these men" (cf. 1 Chronicles 11:19). This meant that by risking their lives they could have died and enjoying the water would have been like drinking their blood or profiting from their death. Jesus thus speaks of our need to delight in the profits of His death, and states further that we need to depend only on Him for our sustenance.

Because He is almighty in power, in paying for the sins of the world, **enough energy was released by His actions on the cross so as to change all of the negative energy back to glorious energy.** In terms of the analogy, this will happen only if we eat his flesh and drink his blood, in other words, partake fully of His sacrifice. And as a result of this sacrifice, we will also see the dawning of new heavens and a new earth. It is therefore true that everlasting life is received and experienced by those who draw from Him. In this regard, He is recorded as having said; "whoever believes in me shall not perish but have everlasting life" (cf. John 3:16). Eating his flesh and drinking His blood is therefore an analogy for believing and trusting in Him. Through faith we thus benefit from his offering. **His love is the tree of life.** We live from His blood, as it is all that reconciles us with God as our Father!

SCIENCE AND JESUS'S BLOOD!

Scientific knowledge that DNA carries life on to later generations fits perfectly with the text; **"the life of the flesh is in the blood"** (Leviticus 17:11). As mentioned previously, the life that is in the blood and leaves when it is shed, was given by the "***breath of lives***", the ***neshamah*** (that we call ***DNA***), breathed in by God. In this way Adam's sin and now corrupted DNA (neshamah or life), was and still is being transferred to all of his descendants. The life in the blood was thus passed on from Adam. Note the following; "The blood in an unborn babies veins is **not** derived from the **mother**... **no blood** flows from the mother to the baby... but is produced within the body of the fetus itself only **after** the introduction of the **male** sperm" (M R De Haan. M.D). DNA or Neshamah thus causes the formation of blood. The first Adam's blood was therefore corrupted and sin by it transmitted through it to all of humanity: "as by **one man** sin entered into the world, and death by sin; and so death **passed upon all** men, for that all have sinned" (Romans 5:12).

Jesus, though, did not have a body/spirit inherited from sinners. Cells from both a man and a woman are needed to produce an offspring and Mary, prior to his birth, never had intercourse with a man. Note that He was the **only** human being ever to be born normally and yet sinless; for Adam and Eve as sinless were created by Him, while Cain and Abel were born after their fall into sin. Due to his birth from Mary, He was of the seed of David according to the flesh, but while a male sperm played no role, blood carrying the Neshamah was a **divine** addition. As conceived by the **Holy Spirit** (cf. Matthew 1: 20,23), He was thus was endowed with **pure neshamah** like Adam in the beginning, and was without sin (cf. Hebrews 4:15); resulting in His blood being also **innocent** and **incorruptible** (cf. Luke 1:35, Matthew 27:4). His blood is "precious (honorable), as of a lamb without blemish or spot" (cf. 1 Peter 1:19). While the first Adam's neshamah became corrupted and transmitted this corruption to all of mankind, neshamah as pure love-energy as entering into ***the last Adam*** by the Holy Spirit (cf. 1 Corinthians 15:45), produced a sinless, innocent and incorruptible life in a soul (NEFESH), so as to give this life to all who adhere to Him. He then gave his soul as an offering for sin (cf. Isaiah 53:10): a **sinless life for corrupt life**, and **pure** blood for **disgraced** blood. His blood cleanses and changes corrupted love-energy back into glorious love-energy. Pure and holy life is in his blood. On "drinking" it, or in this case, believing in Him, His Spirit **restores** our DNA (neshamah) to everlasting life (cf. John 3:16). He is indeed "the Beginning; firstborn from the dead", the ***launch*** of new life (cf. Colossians 1:18).

Only He could have done it; as having almighty power, He could bear the full wrath of God against all of humanity's sin. Like a blade of grass in an oven, a normal man would have fizzed away long before even being able to atone for **one** man's sin. "God sending his own Son in the likeness of sinful flesh, and for sin, condemned sin in the flesh" (Romans 8:3). The word "**condemned**" means that He had **destroyed** sin (cf. 2 Peter 2:6); His sacrifice has broken its power and it can no longer be condemned and punished in believers. We are thus justified by his righteousness which has been imputed to us. **In this sacrifice, He exerted enough love-energy so as to wipe the slate clean.**

Note that Jesus' becoming man and His suffering directly resulted from the "collapse of glory". As Creator (cf. John 1:3), He took on our collapsed state, entered into weak human form, and was in body and spirit subjected to all the anguish we deserved. Although perfect, He became "in all things like unto us, yet without sin" (cf. Hebrews 4:15), subjecting glory to the full curse on the fall. "He, being in the form of God... made himself of no reputation... took the form of a servant... humbled Himself unto death... had no form or comeliness; no beauty that we should desire him" (cf. Philippians 2:6-8, Isaiah 53:2); all glory had been broken!. During the fall, **glory** had been totally **broken** and replaced by decay and suffering, and now He had to bear our curse and wipe it away. As seen previously, the fact that man consists of flesh and blood and is subject to death, results from sin. Blood is thus a symbol of the corruption caused by sin. The fact that He shed His blood and gave His life for ours, means that He took all of the consequences of sin onto Himself.

TO CONCLUDE!

Can anyone still defend evolution or say that the Bible is not true? To repeat what was said previously: **when you examine something from all angles, consider all the possibilities, and are able to counter any arguments opposing it time and again, always arriving at the same conclusion, science accepts it as truth!** There can only be **one** truth for our existence! In a similar manner you may describe a painting either by its **contents**, or by the **message** it conveys, the Bible and science just define this **single** truth from different angles.

Ponder once again the evidence we have provided:

God's original creation can no longer be seen as it no longer exists. The theory of evolution does not at all consider the reality of man's sinfulness (the fall), and what really happened to the universe. All of true existence was changed at His words: "cursed is the ground for thy sake" (Genesis 3:17). Had we seen the original creation, we would have been able to compare it with our present situation and would clearly see that what we now experience is neither what God created, nor the result of evolutionary development.

While science works with the logical laws involving energy, evolution does not consider them at all. They reduce everything to ***chance*** and ***spontaneous*** actions. For example, evolution simplistically argues that life started out as atoms grouping together, and in a pathetic way, simply ignores the complexity of quantum physics, DNA, the laws of Thermodynamics and other scientific processes. They also ignore the undeniable complexity of man's spirit and the body-spirit unity, and cannot explain the origin of man's spirit, his emotions or emotional pain, the uniqueness of human and animal personalities and the differences between sinful and good persons. Their ideas also contradict the laws which make life possible and keep everything exactly in place, such as the laws of physics, the Genetic code, DNA, entropy and resulting suffering and death.

The age of the earth can in no way be proven, but evolutionists just blindly accept it as extremely old. Their theories do not throw any real light either on man's past or his future. They cannot explain why life is on earth and argue against the laws of thermo-dynamics which state that the earth should have disintegrated after 15 billion years, and have no views on eternity.

Is it not a sin in itself that the theory of evolution ignores the concept of true love, not to mention God as Love? Evolution is therefore actually a heartless theory which is as cold as death, promising nothing for eternity. It presents a meaningless existence that just ends in destruction. It is actually amusing that a theory that **can answer no important questions** on life, can occupy people's minds to such a degree, and notwithstanding all its contradictions, be simply accepted. The reason for this is obvious; **they simply don't want to acknowledge God!**

* * *

Gratitude is expressed to Jimmy Henderson for editing the English version of the book, as well as all authors listed as 'Sources', whose work is humbly acknowledged.

SOURCES

Scriptural quotations are from the King James Version. Besides the books listed, several commentaries on the Bible have also been used.

AKAHANE H, T. FURUNO, H. MIYAJIMA, T. YOSH IKAWA, and S. YAMAMOTO, 2004. Rapid wood silicification in hot spring water: An explanation of silicification of wood during the Earth's history, Sedimentary Geology, vol. 169, pp. 219-228.

ALBERTS, LOUW. 1997. Geloof versus Wetenskap. C.U.M. Vereeniging.

ASHTON, J. 1999. In Six Days–Why 50 scientists choose to believe in creation. New Holland publishers Pty. Ltd. Australia.

Bavinck, H. 1967. Gereformeerde Dogmatiek. J.H.Kok. Kampen.

BERKOUWER, G.C. 1952. De Persoon van Christus. J.H.Kok. Kampen.
1951. De algemene openbaring. J.H.Kok. Kampen.
1958. De Zonde I en II . J.H.Kok. Kampen.
1957. De Mens het Beeld Gods. J.H.Kok. Kampen.
1949. Geloof en rechtvaardiging. J.H.Kok, Kampen.

BOOTH, N. 1995. Exploring the solar system. Reed International Books. Hong Kong.

Bromily, G.W. 1974. Theological dictionary of the New Testament. William B. Eerdmans publishing Company.

Custance, A. 1977. Time and Eternity. Zondervan Publishing Company.

DAVIES, P. 1983. God and the new physics. Penguin books. Clays Limited.

DEMBSKI, W. 1998. Mere Creation.–Science, faith and intelligent design. Intervarsity press. Illinois.

Dorean, C. 2011. The Logos Code, Chris Dorean; Feather Communications.

Elliott, M. 1973. Feel, the power of listening to your heart, Tyndale House publishers, Illinois.

FRAIR, W and DAVIS, P. 1994. A Case for creation. Accelerated Christian Education inc. Texas.

HAM, K. Sarfati, J en Wieland, C. 2000. The revised and extended answers book. Ed. D. Batten. Master Books, Creation Ministries International.

HAWKING, Stephen. W. 1990. A Brief History of time. Guild Publishing. London.

HAYWARD, A. 1978. Does God exist? Marshall, Morgan and Scott. Hants. U.K.

Kittel, G. 1965. Theological Dictionary of the N.T. WM. B. Eerdmans, Grand Rapids, Michigan.

MOORE, P. 1994. Atlas of the universe. Reed International books. London.

RICHARDS, L.O. 1989. It couldn't just happen. Word Publishers. Melbourne.

ROSS, HUGH. 1989. The Fingerprint of God. Promise Publishing Co. 1993. The Creator and the Cosmos. Navpress.

SARFATI, J. 1999. Refuting evolution. Master Books. Arizona.

SIEVER, R. 1972. Ed. K. Wedepohl. Handbook of Geochemistry, New York.

SMIT. J van R. 1972. Die Magtige Atoom. Human en Rossouw. Cape Town.

SNELLING, A.A., 1995. Instant petrified wood. Creation, vol. 17, no. 4, pp. 38-40.

STROBEL, Lee. 1998. The Case for Christ. Zondervan. Grand Rapids.

TAYLOR, PAUL S. 1991. The illustrated origins answer book. Eden Productions. Arizona.

THOMPSON, B. 1999. The many faces and causes of unbelief. Apologetics Press, Inc. Montgomery, Alabama.

2001. The origin, nature and destiny of the soul. Apologetics Press, Montgomery, Alabama.

1999. The Bible and the age of the world. Apologetics Press, Inc. Montgomery, Alabama.

1999. The Global Flood of Noah. Apologetics Press, Inc. Montgomery, Alabama.

2003. The case For the Existence of God. Apologetics Press, Inc. Montgomery, Alabama.

1986. The Scientific Case For Creation. Apologetics Press, Inc., Alabama.

BLURP.......

This book unfolds the deepest truths on both man's origin and that of the universe. Should you not read it, you should actually take no further part in any discussion regarding Science, the Bible and evolution. That God IS love means that everything has Love as Architect: was created BY Love to BE love. The reason that we don't experience it this way is because things were not created as we see them. What we now experience was brought about by one fact that is mostly overlooked.

It may come as a surprise, but this book shows how the teachings of Science and the Bible complement each other. In dealing with the same world, they simply have to correspond. The Bible is proven true because of its agreement with science, and science validated because it agrees with the Bible. Both also uncover how laughable the theory of evolution and idea of a 'Big Bang' is! You will further learn:

* That everything consists of energy, and what sub-atomic particles which science calls strange, up, colour, etc., seeming to do what they like, as well as the Higgs-Boson or "God particle", tell us.

* How the breath of life, breathed into man by God, relates to DNA, and the real origin of the Genetic Code.
* How a correct understanding of the connection between Time and Eternity rules out the possibility of evolution, and why the age of the Earth as accepted by evolutionists, cannot be confirmed by radiometric tests or the speed of light.
* How the laws of Thermo-dynamics underscore the Bible!
* How man as a body-spirit is a unity and what happens to this and all of energy at death?

ABOUT THE AUTHOR

Chris Dorean (pseudonym) is a Bible-believer eager to convince you that there is only one basic truth to life, as proven true by both the Bible and Science. Although not formally educated in science, he engages himself in its study. "Dorean" in Greek refers to a free gift; which is what life is. He sees this book as a contribution towards the ongoing discourse on the Bible and science.

CPSIA information can be obtained
at www.ICGtesting.com
Printed in the USA
LVOW13s1718070217
523494LV00011B/1018/P